CIVIL RIGHTS MOVEMENT

Martin Luther King Jr. and the 1963 March on Washington

CIVIL RIGHTS MOVEMENT

Martin Luther King Jr. and the 1963 March on Washington

David Aretha

Greensboro, North Carolina

Civil Rights Movement
Martin Luther King Jr.
and the 1963 March on Washington
Copyright © 2013 by Morgan Reynolds Publishing

Library of Congress Cataloging-in-Publication Data

Aretha, David.
  Martin Luther King Jr. and the 1963 March on Washington / by David
Aretha.
      pages cm
  Includes bibliographical references.
  ISBN 978-1-59935-372-2 -- ISBN 978-1-59935-373-9 (e-book) (print) 1.
King, Martin Luther, Jr., 1929-1968--Juvenile literature. 2. March on
Washington for Jobs and Freedom (1963 : Washington, D.C.)--Juvenile
literature. 3. Civil rights demonstrations--Washington
(D.C.)--History--20th century--Juvenile literature. 4. African
Americans--Civil rights--Juvenile literature. I. Title.
  E185.97.K5A84 2014
  323.092--dc23
  [B]
                              2012035355

PRINTED IN THE UNITED STATES OF AMERICA
First Edition

Book cover and interior designed by:
Ed Morgan, navyblue design studio
Greensboro, NC

CONTENTS

"I've Been 'Buked and I've Been Scorned"

I'VE BEEN 'BUKED AND I'VE BEEN SCORNED,
I'VE BEEN 'BUKED AND I'VE BEEN SCORNED,
CHILDREN
I'VE BEEN 'BUKED AND I'VE BEEN SCORNED
TRYIN' TO MAKE THIS JOURNEY ALL ALONE

Gospel singer Mahalia Jackson sang this spiritual at the
Lincoln Memorial before Dr. Martin Luther King Jr. gave
his famous "I Have a Dream" speech.

CHAPTER ONE

GROWING UP WITH JIM CROW

When Martin Luther King Jr. was a small child in the 1930s, his father—the pastor of Ebenezer Church in Atlanta—took him to a downtown shoe store. After they sat down in the front of the store, a young white clerk approached them.

"I'll be happy to wait on you if you'll just move to those seats in the rear," the clerk said.

Normally a mild-mannered man, Reverend King took offense to the racial slight. He told the clerk that he and his son were comfortable where they were.

"Sorry," the clerk said, "but you'll have to move."

"We'll either buy shoes sitting here," King retorted, "or we won't buy shoes at all."

At that point, Reverend King grabbed his son's hand and led him out the door. The boy had never seen his father look so angry. Years later, Martin Jr. would write: "I still remember walking down the street beside him as he muttered, 'I don't care how long I have to live with this system, I will never accept it.'"

Some thirty years after the shoe store incident, Martin Luther King Jr. delivered his "I Have a Dream" speech at the 1963 March on Washington for Jobs and Freedom. It was the first major step toward bridging America's racial divide—a chasm that had endured through two hundred years of slavery and a hundred more years of Jim Crow segregation.

The 1963 demonstration was called the March on Washington for *Jobs and Freedom* because African Americans were lacking in both. Though President Abraham Lincoln had issued the Emancipation Proclamation—freeing the slaves—on January 1, 1863, white America continued to deny rights and liberties to black Americans for the next hundred years.

From 1865 to 1870, the U.S. Congress passed the Thirteenth, Fourteenth, and Fifteenth amendments, which, respectively, abolished slavery, granted citizenship to everyone who had been or would be born in the United States, and guaranteed voting rights to all adult males. But white Southerners were not willing to eradicate a racial caste system that had benefited them since the 1600s. For generations, the southern economy had relied on free black labor. To justify their enslavement (and, after the Civil War, oppression) of black people, whites perpetuated a myth that blacks were mentally, emotionally, and even spiritually inferior. Many considered those of African descent to be subhuman. "Boy," "coon," and "nigger" were just some of the pejoratives that whites used to make black people feel humiliated and "in their place."

With "black codes" in the 1860s and '70s and then Jim Crow (segregation) laws up through the 1960s, local and state governments in the South placed severe restrictions on black Americans. Schools, streetcars, buses, drinking fountains, restrooms, theaters, pools, restaurants, and many other public facilities were segregated. When the U.S. Supreme Court ruled in 1896 that "separate but equal" facilities were acceptable, it gave the green light to perpetuate separate (segregated) facilities.

Simply by separating facilities into black and white, whites made blacks feel both different and inferior. Making matters worse, the black facilities were hardly ever "equal" to whites'.

A segregated bus station in Memphis, Tennessee, prominently displays a "White Waiting Room" sign in this 1943 photo.

They were almost always inferior, particularly the dilapidated, grossly underfunded public schools that black children struggled to learn in.

Because of expensive poll taxes, impossible-to-pass literacy/civics tests, and strong intimidation, relatively few southern blacks were registered to vote. Black Americans could be arrested for the slightest offense, especially if they challenged white authority—or, God forbid, had sexual or even flirtatious relations with white women. Hundreds of black men were lynched for violating—or just being rumored to have violated—this taboo. In southern courtrooms, the fate of black defendants was determined by white prosecutors, white judges, and all-white juries.

In the rural South, whites kept most black citizens economically enslaved. Through sharecropping, black men rented land from plantation owners. Blacks got to harvest and sell crops, but they owed so much money to the plantation owners—for rent, food, farming equipment, and so on—that they were chronically in debt to their employers.

In southern and northern cities, black citizens had little opportunity to prosper. Public schools in black neighborhoods were rarely properly funded, meaning the education was inferior. Black families had little money to begin with, meaning few could afford tuition for higher education or a down payment on a house. In the nice city and suburban neighborhoods—those with good public schools and escalating property values—white homeowners and real estate agents often gave black home shoppers the cold shoulder.

Employment was an issue even in the North. Government agencies, businesses, and unions tended to freeze out black workers. A slogan in the South during the Great Depression was "No jobs for niggers until every white man has a job." Throughout the country, the rate of black unemployment was roughly twice as high as white unemployment. In some cities during the peak of the Depression, black unemployment exceeded 50 percent.

In the first half of the twentieth century, a number of civil rights advocates fought against the injustice. The National Association for the Advancement of Colored People (NAACP) focused largely on anti-lynching legislation and then the destruction of segregated school systems. In the 1930s, New York activist Adam Clayton Powell organized the "Don't Buy Where You Can't Work" campaign. And for decades, labor leader Asa Philip Randolph fought for better working conditions for black workers.

Born in Florida in 1889, Randolph was the son of strong-willed parents—a minister and a seamstress. Randolph remembered the night when his mother stood on guard at their home with a shotgun while his father ventured to the local jail to stop a white mob from lynching a black man. Tall, handsome, and determined, Asa became the valedictorian of his senior class in high school. Randolph was a socialist, as reflected in his words: "A community is democratic only when the humblest and weakest person can enjoy the highest civil, economic, and social rights that the biggest and most powerful possess."

For most of his life, Randolph focused his attention on improving working conditions for black employees. In 1925, he formed the Brotherhood of Sleeping Car Porters. These black railroad employees were underpaid and overworked, but over time Randolph was able to negotiate for higher salaries and shorter workweeks.

In 1941, as one of the most prominent labor leaders and civil rights activists in the nation, Randolph took on the United States government. He threatened to stage a massive demonstration in Washington unless President Franklin Roosevelt banned racial discrimination in the defense industry. Randolph and his supporters created a March on Washington committee, which was supported by the NAACP and the National Urban League. Through black newspapers and black churches, they drummed up support for the proposed march, which they envisioned would include tens of thousands of protesters.

With plans for the march underway, New York mayor Fiorello La Guardia and First Lady Eleanor Roosevelt persuaded Randolph and NAACP leader Walter White to talk to President Roosevelt. Both the mayor and first lady knew that previous marches on Washington had not been pleasant. In August 1925, 35,000 Ku Klux Klan members paraded through the nation's capital. And in June 1932, 15,000 to 20,000 World War I veterans marched on

Fifty thousand white-robed Klansmen march down Pennsylvania Avenue in Washington, D.C., in 1925.

Washington demanding money that was due to them. Thousands of out-of-work veterans and their families set up tents and remained there for weeks until President Herbert Hoover ordered the Army to remove them. Two babies died and hundreds of people were injured. "[T]he whole scene," wrote Major Dwight Eisenhower, "was pitiful."

Not wanting to deal with thousands of angry marchers, especially during wartime, President Roosevelt made a decision that appeased Randolph. The president established the Fair Employment Practices Committee, which forbade racial discrimination in the defense industry. In turn, Randolph called off the march.

Black activists would lament that the ruling did not apply to the military forces, which would remain segregated throughout World War II. However, Roosevelt's action was one of the first significant civil rights actions taken by the federal government in the twentieth century—thanks largely to Randolph's aggressiveness. Randolph understood that a march on Washington, or even the threat of one, was a mighty weapon in the arsenal of black activists. The White House and Congress would always be wary of an enormous gathering of disgruntled African Americans "besieging" their neighborhood. While there would be no march on Washington in 1941, Randolph would continue to look for the opportunity to make one happen.

Up through the mid-1950s, civil rights gains were sporadic. The Congress of Racial Equality (CORE) staged the first sit-ins and "freedom rides" in the 1940s. Major League Baseball finally integrated in 1947, as the courageous Jackie Robinson made a splash with the Brooklyn Dodgers. A year later, President Harry Truman signed an executive order integrating the military. And in 1953, residents in Baton Rouge, Louisiana, staged a boycott of the city's bus system.

The civil rights movement kicked off in earnest on May 17, 1954, when the U.S. Supreme Court ruled that segregated public schooling was unconstitutional. Some school systems, most notably in Baltimore, Maryland, and Washington, D.C., quickly adhered to the historic ruling, but most southern governments refused to desegregate. (Many would defy the order into the 1960s and beyond.) The high court's decision inflamed tensions in the South, with segregationists referring to May 17 as Black Monday. The White Citizens' Council, with branches across the South, used economic retaliation against those who supported desegregation measures.

Within this hostile climate, fourteen-year-old Emmett Till, an African American from Chicago, was brutally murdered by two men in Mississippi. "I'm going to make an example of you," said J. W. Milam before he killed Till, "just so everybody can know how me and my folks stand." The Till murder and the subsequent trial, in which an all-white jury ruled that the two men were innocent, riled up African Americans and righteous whites throughout the country.

In early 1955, Martin Luther King was not yet a public figure. King had graduated from Morehouse College with a degree in sociology at age nineteen in 1944. Like his father, he followed a religious path, earning a bachelor of divinity degree from Crozer Theological Seminary in Pennsylvania in 1951. He married Coretta Scott two years later, and in 1955 he became the pastor of Dexter Avenue Baptist Church in Montgomery, Alabama. In June 1955, King received a doctorate in philosophy from Boston University.

While King's primary focus was theology, he had a strong interest in the plight of his fellow African Americans. He was greatly influenced by the book *Jesus and the Disinherited*, authored by one of his mentors, theologian and civil rights activist Howard Thurman. *Jesus and the Disinherited* demonstrated how the Gospel could be used as a manual of resistance for the poor and neglected.

In his early days at Dexter Avenue Baptist Church, King was not the rousing "civil rights" preacher that America would come to know. At Dexter on January 24, 1954, for example, he delivered a sermon that he had written entitled "The Dimensions of a Complete Life." The sermon was deeply theological, difficult to understand, and, many would say, dry. "So much of the noblest life which we have seen," he preached, "both collective and individual, dissatisfies us with its partialness."

At the time, King's primary ambitions were serving his flock at Dexter and attending to his family; his first child, Yolanda, was born on November 17, 1955. But fourteen days after King became a father, an incident occurred on a city bus in Montgomery that would dramatically change his life—and the course of America—forever.

"Ain't Gonna Let Nobody Turn Me Around"

AIN'T GONNA LET NOBODY TURN ME 'ROUND,
TURN ME ROUND, TURN ME 'ROUND.
AIN'T GONNA LET NOBODY, TURN ME 'ROUND.
I'M GONNA KEEP ON A-WALKIN', KEEP ON A-TALKIN',
WALKIN' INTO FREEDOM LAND.
AIN'T GONNA LET SEGREGATION TURN ME 'ROUND,
TURN ME 'ROUND, TURN ME 'ROUND.
AIN'T GONNA LET SEGREGATION TURN ME 'ROUND,
I'M GONNA KEEP ON A-WALKIN', KEEP ON A-TALKIN'.
WALKIN' INTO FREEDOM LAND.

Reverend Ralph Abernathy taught this song, which is based on an old spiritual, "Don't Let Nobody Turn Me Round," to a gathering at a Baptist church in Albany during the summer of 1962. It quickly caught on, and student protesters often sang it during mass arrests and demonstrations.

CHAPTER TWO

THE FIGHT FOR CIVIL RIGHTS

Four days after Rosa Parks refused to give up her seat to a white man on a Montgomery bus, the black citizens of that Alabama city staged a bus boycott. Martin Luther King had helped initiate the protest, and on that morning, December 5, 1955, he witnessed the fruits of their labor.

"I was in the kitchen drinking my coffee," King wrote, "when I heard Coretta cry, 'Martin, Martin, come quickly!' I put down my cup and ran toward the living room. As I approached the front window Coretta pointed joyfully to a slowly moving bus: 'Darling, it's empty!' I could hardly believe what I saw."

With the one-day boycott a spectacular success, King enthusiastically immersed himself into the civil rights struggle. Later that day, he accepted the position of president of the Montgomery Improvement Association (MIA), meaning he would oversee the bus boycott that would last 381 days.

That very night, a great throng of African Americans descended upon Holt Street Baptist Church for a meeting about the boycott. King had just minutes to prepare a speech that would be broadcast through amplifiers to the 10,000 or so black citizens who surrounded the church. Those in attendance witnessed the emergence of a powerful speechmaker and charismatic leader.

"You know, my friends, there comes a time when people get tired of being trampled over by the iron feet of oppression," King intoned. He overflowed with emotion as he declared: "There comes a time when people get tired of being plunged across the abyss of humiliation, where they'd experience the bleakness of nagging despair. There comes a time when people get tired of being pushed out of the glittering sunlight of life's July and left standing amid the piercing chill of an alpine November. There comes a time."

The crowd erupted in applause and stomped on the wooden floors. A star was born.

Much of what happened at the 1963 March on Washington had its roots in Montgomery. Were it not for Parks and the bus boycott, King might not have become a national figure. Moreover, one of the famous lines in "I Have a Dream"—"justice runs down like water and righteousness like a mighty stream"—was also in King's December 5 speech. In addition, March on Washington leaders A. Philip Randolph and Bayard Rustin contributed their organizing expertise to the Montgomery boycott.

Black citizens endured considerable hardship during the boycott, as whites retaliated with arrests, harassment, and sometimes violence. On January 30, 1956, King's house was bombed. But the boycott achieved its organizers' goals. Montgomery officials agreed to desegregate the city's buses, and the U.S. Supreme Court ruled that segregation on intrastate buses was unconstitutional.

Looking to expand the fight for civil rights, southern black ministers formed the Southern Christian Leadership Conference (SCLC), with King as president. The SCLC's first initiative was the Crusade for Citizenship, which was launched with the Prayer Pilgrimage to Washington, D.C., on May 17, 1957—the third anniversary of the *Brown v. Board of Education* decision.

In some ways, the Prayer Pilgrimage for Freedom was a prequel to the March on Washington. Randolph and his trusted colleague, Rustin, organized both events, and the SCLC and NAACP played strong roles in each. Both demonstrations were staged in front of the Lincoln Memorial, and Mahalia Jackson sang at both.

At the Prayer Pilgrimage, some 25,000 people descended on the nation's capital, placing it among the largest gatherings ever in Washington to that point. The demonstration focused on enforcing the *Brown* ruling and on voting rights. In some areas in the South, less than 10 percent of African Americans were registered to vote, largely because of the exclusionary and intimidation tactics of southern whites.

Dressed in a preacher's robe and standing beside an American flag, King addressed the enormous crowd with his "Give Us the Ballot" speech. "Give us the ballot," he declared, "and we will transfer the salient misdeeds of bloodthirsty mobs into the calculated good deeds of orderly citizens. . . . Give us the ballot, and we will quietly and nonviolently, without rancor or bitterness, implement the Supreme Court's decision of May 17th, 1954. . . ." The people responded with chants of "Give us the ballot!"

Bayard Rustin's contributions to this event and the civil rights movement as a whole should not be ignored. The son of activists, Rustin lived his life on the fringes of society. He was a member of the Young Communist League during the 1930s, was a pacifist even during World War II, and was openly gay. In 1942, the year he helped found the Congress of Racial Equality (a major civil rights organization), Rustin deliberately sat in the white section of a bus to defy segregation. He was arrested and beaten.

From leaders of the Gandhian movement, Rustin learned nonviolent-resistance techniques in India, and he passed along such wisdom to American activists. Rustin helped King organize the SCLC, and before that he advised the young preacher on nonviolence in Montgomery. *Nonviolence* would become an integral component of the civil rights movement and synonymous with King himself.

King, however, did not have many friends in the White House in the late 1950s. Outside of sending in the National Guard to escort students to class at Little Rock Central High School in 1957, President Dwight Eisenhower was largely ambivalent to the cause of civil rights. The 1957 Civil Rights Act—the first civil rights act in eighty-two years—established a Commission on Civil Rights in the executive branch and a civil rights division within the Justice Department. However, the 1957 act and the 1960 Civil Rights Act did little to achieve their primary intention: ending voter disenfranchisement in the Jim Crow South.

Like thousands of others in the movement, King kept the pressure on. In 1958, he wrote his first book, *Stride Toward Freedom*, and was nearly killed when stabbed by a deranged African American woman in New York City. A year later, he visited India to study Gandhi's philosophy of nonviolence. In the early 1960s, he led protests, was arrested multiple times, and laid witness to a burnt cross on his front lawn.

Between the Montgomery bus boycott and the March on Washington, the Greensboro Four sit-in may have been the most significant event of the civil rights movement. On February 1, 1960, four black North Carolina A&T College students—Ezell Blair, Franklin McCain, David Richmond, and Joseph McNeil—sat down at the white lunch counter at Woolworth's. After their request for coffee was turned down, the foursome remained seated until the store closed. The next day, twenty-seven protesters were refused service at the white counter, and the following day three hundred protesters arrived.

Ronald Martin, Robert Patterson, and Mark Martin stage a sit-down strike after being refused service at a F. W. Woolworth luncheon counter, in Greensboro, North Carolina, in 1960.

Sit-in protests went viral across the South and other parts of the country. By September 1961, according to the Southern Regional Council, some 70,000 people in one hundred cities in twenty states had been involved in sit-in demonstrations, with 3,600 of them arrested. Up through the mid-1960s, these passive-resistance protests occurred at restaurants, movie theaters, libraries, hotels, museums, pools, beaches, golf courses, amusement parks, and other types of places that were segregated. Of those who were arrested, many staged "jail-ins," in which they refused to post bail. Many of these protests were successful. Either to avoid future troubles or because it was the right thing to do, many business owners and civic leaders desegregated their facilities.

Martin Luther King didn't know the Greensboro Four, but he did influence them. At least one of them had read a copy of *Martin Luther King and the Montgomery Story,* and in 1958 Blair and Richmond had heard King speak at Bennett College in Greensboro. Blair said the speech had gotten his heart thumping and that tears had welled up in his eyes.

King himself got caught up in the sit-in craze. In October 1960, he was arrested in Atlanta for participating in a lunch counter sit-in. While in custody, he was convicted for violating probation by driving in Georgia with an Alabama license. His sentence: four months of hard labor at Reidsville State Prison. Fortunately for King, Robert F. Kennedy persuaded Georgia authorities to release him.

Martin Luther King Jr., accompanied by Lonnie King (*left*) and an unidentified woman, walks by a segregation protester following his October 9, 1960, arrest in Atlanta.

Days later, Robert's older brother was elected president. John F. Kennedy, a progressive Democrat, claimed that "the torch has been passed to a new generation of Americans." But those who thought that Kennedy would blaze a path of glory for African Americans were sadly mistaken. JFK had barely won the 1960 election over Richard Nixon, and he feared that most of the southern states—which had been predominantly Democratic—would go Republican if he cracked down hard on segregation. Kennedy would eventually take strong steps against racial injustice, but not until 1963.

Freedom Rides were the big civil rights event in 1961. After the U.S. Supreme Court ruled that segregation in interstate bus terminal facilities was unconstitutional, busloads of Freedom Riders set out to test the ruling. Some of these black and white activists were beaten by white mobs in the South, and in Anniston, Alabama, one of their buses was firebombed. Again, King was heavily involved. In Montgomery on May 21, 1961, King and 1,200 people inside the First Baptist Church were besieged by 3,000 whites, who threw rocks through the church's windows and set cars on fire. Again, Robert Kennedy, now the U.S. attorney general, came to the rescue by telling the Alabama governor to call in the National Guard.

By early 1962, the civil rights movement hit a roadblock in Albany, Georgia. During the previous November, members of the Student Nonviolent Coordinating Committee (SNCC) initiated a protest against segregation in a city in which 20,000 African Americans were treated as second-class citizens. Hundreds of activists participated in marches, boycotts, sit-ins, jail-ins, and Freedom Rides. In the first two weeks of the protests, five hundred people were arrested.

On December 15, King arrived to participate in the Albany campaign. That night at Shiloh Baptist Church, he rallied the protesters with another inspiring speech. "Don't stop now," he urged them. "Keep moving. Don't get weary. We will wear them down with our capacity to suffer."

A Greyhound bus goes up in flames after an angry mob in Alabama set it on fire.

Unfortunately for the protesters, the efforts of their nine-month campaign were largely in vain. The main objective of citywide protests was to garner nationwide empathy. Televised images of orderly protests, they reasoned, would have a positive but small effect on the national consciousness. But film of police officers and segregationists bullying or attacking protesters would generate far more publicity and national outrage, which in theory would prompt the public and federal government to call for strong civil rights legislation.

That didn't happen in Albany, largely because savvy Chief of Police Laurie Pritchett made sure that he and his officers kept their cool. When King and his close colleague, Reverend Ralph Abernathy, were jailed in July 1962, an unknown person bailed them out, reportedly to avoid the publicity of King being behind bars. "I've been thrown out of lots of places in my day," Abernathy quipped, "but never before have I been thrown out of jail."

An incident in Oxford, Mississippi, in the early fall of 1962 illustrated how resistant the South was to integration. In his efforts to become the first black student ever at the University of Mississippi, James Meredith arrived with an entourage of one hundred federal marshals, three hundred U.S. border guards, and one hundred prison guards. But that wasn't nearly enough to quell the 3,000 whites who rioted on campus. President Kennedy had to intervene, and 23,000 soldiers were called in to end the rioting.

During the mayhem, Kennedy addressed the nation from the White House. Instead of chastising Mississippians for flagrant bigotry, the president seemingly tried to sweet-talk them into ending the violence. "Mississippi and her University, moreover, are noted for their courage, for their contribution of talent and thought to the affairs of this nation . . . ," he said. "You have a great tradition to uphold, a tradition of honor and courage won on the field of battle and on the gridiron as well as the University campus. You have a new opportunity to show that you are men of patriotism and integrity."

The civil rights movement was certainly at a low point in late 1962. Besides the Meredith fiasco and the failures in Albany, the conditions of African Americans remained abysmal. In Mississippi in 1960, only 6.7 percent of black citizens were registered to vote. In 1962, five counties in that state with a majority black population had zero black registrants. In 1960, six years after the *Brown* ruling, only 0.2 percent of black students in the South were going to school with whites. And according to the U.S. Census, 55.1 percent of African Americans lived in poverty in 1959, compared to 18.1 percent of whites.

In the fall of 1962, A. Philip Randolph suggested to friend Bayard Rustin another march on Washington, with this one focused on jobs. Randolph, a labor expert, believed that African Americans could never advance as a people until they improved their employment situation. At the time, the black unemployment rate across the country was roughly twice that of whites and their earnings were approximately half as much.

Unafraid of frigid weather, Randolph wanted to stage the event on January 1, 1963, the one hundredth anniversary of Lincoln's Emancipation Proclamation. He would call the event the Emancipation March for Jobs. Randolph, however, could not get the support of King and the major civil rights leaders, even after he changed the name to the March on Washington for Jobs and Freedom. King and the SCLC were in the midst of planning a protest campaign in Birmingham, Alabama. Birmingham, known as the most segregated city in America, would require a full-blown, nonviolent assault.

On January 14, 1963, a new civil rights foe was sworn in as governor of Alabama. "Segregation now," George Wallace declared during his inauguration speech, "segregation tomorrow, and segregation forever!"

It was clear that the civil rights movement would need a full arsenal to destroy Jim Crow. In 1963, the two biggest weapons would be the campaign in Birmingham and, a few months later, the March on Washington.

"Lift Every Voice and Sing"

LIFT EV'RY VOICE AND SING,
TILL EARTH AND HEAVEN RING,
RING WITH THE HARMONIES OF LIBERTY;
LET OUR REJOICING RISE
HIGH AS THE LIST'NING SKIES,
LET IT RESOUND LOUD AS THE ROLLING SEA.
SING A SONG FULL OF THE FAITH THAT THE DARK PAST
HAS TAUGHT US,
SING A SONG FULL OF THE HOPE THAT THE PRESENT
HAS BROUGHT US;
FACING THE RISING SUN OF OUR NEW DAY BEGUN,
LET US MARCH ON TILL VICTORY IS WON.

Written as a poem by James Weldon Johnson (1871–1938) and set to
music by his brother James Rosamond Johnson (1873–1954) in 1900,
"Lift Every Voice and Sing" is often called the "Black National Anthem,"
the "Negro National Anthem" or the "African American Anthem."

CHAPTER THREE
"THERE *WILL* BE A **MARCH**"

History books duly note that the Birmingham campaign and the March on Washington were two seminal events in American history. But rarely do they mention that the two were linked together. In fact, if it weren't for events in Birmingham, the March on Washington might never have occurred.

The Birmingham campaign was known as "Project C"—for confrontation. Activists expected a bloody battleground. Because of the frequent dynamite attacks by the Ku Klux Klan, black residents had nicknamed Alabama's largest city "Bombingham." On two occasions, local minister Fred Shuttlesworth had witnessed the bombing of his house, and whites had beaten him multiple times. The fiery activist headed the Alabama Christian Movement for Human Rights, which teamed on Project C with Martin Luther King's SCLC.

By this point, King had become such a revered figure and orator that he could charge money for speaking at events. He inevitably forwarded the funds to the civil rights cause. In March 1963, King delivered a series of speeches throughout the country simply to raise money for the bail that activists would undoubtedly need during the Birmingham campaign.

The campaign's "Birmingham Manifesto" called for the desegregation of all businesses and demanded fair-hiring practices in the city. Public Safety Commissioner Eugene "Bull" Connor led the opposition. The sixty-five-year-old Connor, a notorious segregationist, was crotchety and short-tempered—just the foil that the SCLC was looking for. Project C began on April 3 with sit-ins in downtown stores. Connor responded by arresting twenty or more demonstrators without incident.

On April 11, King and Shuttlesworth were served an injunction that barred civil rights leaders from leading any demonstration in the city. Deliberately defying the order, King and Ralph Abernathy led a march on Good Friday. They were arrested. While in solitary confinement, King wrote a response to white clergymen who had denounced the demonstrations as "unwise and untimely." This "Letter From a Birmingham Jail" is one of King's most acclaimed writings.

Ralph Abernathy (*left*) and Martin Luther King Jr. lead a group of demonstrators as they march toward city hall in Birmingham, Alabama.

Writing on newspaper margins and scraps of paper, King began with a formal response as to why the SCLC was taking direct action in Birmingham instead of engaging in "honest and open negotiation in our area," as the clergymen had urged. But in the middle of the letter, King unleashed a personal, emotional response about why, "after more than 340 years," black Americans were sick and tired of waiting for justice. Referring largely to his own experiences, he wrote:

when you suddenly find your tongue twisted and your speech stammering as you seek to explain to your six-year-old daughter why she can't go to the public amusement park that has just been advertised on television, and see tears welling up in her eyes when she is told that Funtown is closed to colored children, and see ominous clouds of inferiority beginning to form in her little mental sky, and see her beginning to distort her personality by developing an unconscious bitterness toward white people; when you have to concoct an answer for a five-year-old son who is asking: "Daddy, why do white people treat colored people so mean?"; when you take a cross-country drive and find it necessary to sleep night after night in the uncomfortable corners of your automobile because no motel will accept you; . . . when you are harried by day and haunted by night by the fact that you are a Negro, living constantly at tiptoe stance, never quite knowing what to expect next, and are plagued with inner fears and outer resentments; when you are forever fighting a degenerating sense of "nobodiness"—then you will understand why we find it difficult to wait.

When King and Abernathy were bailed out of jail on April 20, they found the Birmingham movement largely stalled. However, young SNCC activist James Bevel had a plan. He wanted to lead hundreds of black elementary and high school students on a march through Birmingham, an event that would certainly capture the nation's attention. While opponents scoffed at the idea of putting children in harm's way, King approved the plan.

Of the one-thousand-plus children who marched on May 2, Connor's men arrested hundreds of them. The next day, officials turned police dogs and powerful fire hoses—strong enough to break a person's ribs—on the young protesters. By this point, Connor had lost all restraint. "All you got to do is tell them you're going to bring the dogs," Connor said. "Look at 'em run. I want to see the dogs work. Look at those niggers run!"

Through May 6, more than 2,000 demonstrators were arrested, with many sent to outdoor jail yards. In a rally at St. Luke's Church that day, King urged Birmingham residents to continue the fight. "In spite of the difficulties—and we are going to have a few more difficulties—keep climbing," he declared. "Keep moving. If you can't fly, run! If you can't run, walk! If you can't walk, crawl! But by all means keep moving."

The shocking images from Birmingham stunned the nation and the world. On college campuses, progressive white students couldn't believe the injustice that was occurring in their country. Gloria Clark remembered watching Bull Connor being interviewed on television: "I've never forgotten this line: 'We can take care of our nigras ourselves.' . . . I said, 'Am I living in the same country with this man?' . . . And I said no way is he going to define how people are treated in the country I live in. No way do I want a man like that defining it."

At the urging of U.S. attorney general Robert Kennedy, the SCLC and Birmingham business leaders brokered an agreement on May 10. The latter agreed to desegregate lunch counters and certain other facilities and to improve hiring practices for black citizens. Governor George Wallace would denounce the deal, and on May 11 bombs exploded at the home of A. D. King (Martin's brother) and at the Gaston Motel, where Martin Luther King had been staying.

Following the violence in Birmingham, which outraged most of his colleagues in Washington, President Kennedy believed it was time to put civil rights at the forefront of his agenda—and soon, because events were happening quickly. On May 20, the U.S. Supreme Court declared that city segregation ordinances were unconstitutional. In Jackson, Mississippi, sit-in activists were being abused by segregationists. As seen in a May 28 photograph, former Jackson police officer Benny Oliver viciously kicked a lunch counter demonstrator as he lay on the floor.

Two days later, King sent a telegram to the president requesting a meeting. King hoped that he could persuade Kennedy to issue an executive order against segregation. That very night, King talked on the phone to SCLC member Stanley Levison, who helped organize fund-raisers and events for King. Because Levison had been a leader of the Communist Party USA in the 1950s, the FBI had wiretapped his phone—which allowed them to record this conversation.

Telling Levison that "we are on a breakthrough," King said it was time for "a mass protest" . . . a "mass march" on Washington. They agreed that to "really push" civil rights legislation, a march of "possibly a hundred thousand people" was necessary. Levison said that A. Philip Randolph would likely contribute to the endeavor. Randolph had already been planning a march but had not yet got the support of the major civil rights groups.

By June, it was apparent that the Kennedy administration was working on a civil rights bill. In a conference call to advisers, King declared that "something dramatic must be done" to support the civil rights bill because "I don't think it will pass otherwise." NAACP leader Roy Wilkins, who was always very careful about not offending leadership in Washington, had rejected Randolph's proposed marches. So King and his advisers came up with this plan: Get Randolph on board first and then announce the march publicly. At that point, Wilkins would have no choice but to go along.

On June 11, Governor George Wallace stood in front of a school building door at the University of Alabama to symbolically prevent Vivian Malone and James Hood from becoming the first black students to attend that school. National Guardsmen escorted them in. That night, President Kennedy addressed the nation with his strongest speech yet in support of civil rights.

Kennedy said that it "ought to be possible for American consumers of any color to receive equal service in places of public accommodation, such as hotels and restaurants and theaters and retail stores, without being forced to resort to demonstrations in the street, and it ought to be possible for American citizens of any color to register and to vote in a free election without interference or fear of reprisal."

Of the tens of millions of Americans who watched the president's speech, many were undoubtedly surprised to hear the statistics that he quoted:

Governor George Wallace attempting to block integration at the University of Alabama

> The Negro baby born in America today . . . has about one-half as much chance of completing high school as a white baby born in the same place on the same day, one-third as much chance of completing college, one-third as much chance of becoming a professional man, twice as much chance of becoming unemployed, about one-seventh as much chance of earning $10,000 a year, a life expectancy which is seven years shorter, and the prospects of earning only half as much.

Freedom, Kennedy said, was for all Americans:

> We preach freedom around the world, and we mean it, and we cherish our freedom here at home, but are we to say to the world, and much more importantly, to each other that this is the land of the free except for the Negroes; that we have no second-class citizens except Negroes; that we have no class or caste system, no ghettoes, no master race except with respect to Negroes? Now the time has come for this nation to fulfill its promise. The events in Birmingham and elsewhere have so increased the cries for equality that no city or state or legislative body can prudently choose to ignore them.

Kennedy's speech was in the spirit of those recited by King, who immediately sent a letter of praise to the president. Martin Luther King was emboldened; the Birmingham campaign had been so successful that it had helped bring the power of the presidency to the civil rights cause.

However, the euphoria of the evening was soon dashed. Medgar Evers, an outspoken NAACP leader in Jackson, was fatally shot in the back by a segregationist on June 11. The next morning, the president learned that southern Democrats in Congress had suddenly rejected a major section of the administration's public works bill. Kennedy realized that, even though they were members of his own party, these Southerners were retaliating against him because of his civil rights speech. House Majority Leader Carl Albert "told the President it would be nearly impossible to pass farm bills or mass-transit funding. On every close question from foreign aid to the space budget, civil rights loomed as the margin of defeat."

In a 1963 Gallup poll of American citizens, civil rights was listed as the most important crisis facing America. In June, President Kennedy probably would have agreed. Demonstrations, arrests, and violent episodes were erupting all over the country, including the arrest of two hundred black children in Savannah, Georgia. On June 14, some 3,000 angry civil rights demonstrators showed up outside Robert Kennedy's office. His attempts to appease the crowd, while speaking through a bullhorn, were met with jeers and boos.

On June 19, the president strongly urged Congress to enact a civil rights act—and quickly, specifically before the congressional recess. Kennedy outlined the issues he wanted to see covered in the new legislation. First of all, voting rights needed to be assured, and constitutionally mandated school desegregation must continue, with federal assistance when necessary. Black citizens needed to have guaranteed access to public facilities, such as restaurants and hotels. Regarding employment, he proposed a three-pronged attack consisting of job creation, training, and the eradication of racial discrimination in hiring.

Attorney General Robert Kennedy speaks to a crowd of African American demonstrators on June 14, 1963.

The president concluded: "In this year of the emancipation centennial, justice requires us to insure the blessings of liberty for all Americans and their posterity—not merely for reasons of economic efficiency, world diplomacy, and domestic tranquility, but above all, because it is right."

Determined to ride the momentum, King announced the next day that a march on Washington was forthcoming. After hearing King's words, Randolph solicited labor colleague Cleveland Robinson to call a press conference in New York City on June 21. Robinson told the media that plans were in the works for a march on Washington.

Events were unfolding quickly. On June 22, King, Randolph, Wilkins, and other civil rights leaders gathered at the White House for a meeting with the president that had been scheduled days earlier. This had all the makings of a contentious meeting, because Kennedy did not want the march. He wanted justice for African Americans because it was the right thing to do and because he needed to calm the growing angst of black citizens across the country. But at the same time, he wanted the process to be orderly so as to limit the backlash he would get from the South. Moreover, the administration was concerned that the demonstration might lead to protests, violence, mass arrests, and, in general, chaos.

When King arrived at the White House, he found himself in an unexpected conversation with U.S. assistant attorney general Burke Marshall. In a serious tone, Marshall told King to sever ties with Stanley Levison, whom Marshall said was a Soviet agent who had infiltrated the civil rights movement. King didn't believe Marshall, who turned the discussion over to his boss, Robert Kennedy. Again, King refused to agree to sever ties with his friend, because he did

A photograph of a White House meeting with civil rights leaders on June 22, 1963. (*Front row*) Martin Luther King Jr., Robert F. Kennedy, Roy Wilkins, and Lyndon Baines Johnson

not believe he was a Communist infiltrator. Robert Kennedy then passed King over to his boss, the president.

Kennedy told King that if word leaked that the civil rights movement was infiltrated by Communists, it would scandalize not only the movement but the administration that was supporting it. "If they shoot *you* down, they'll shoot *us* down, too," Kennedy told King. "So we're asking you to be careful." The conversation concluded with King asking Kennedy for proof about Levison, and the president agreed to provide it.

King had a feeling that this wasn't about Levison. In reality, it was largely about King himself. FBI director J. Edgar Hoover had been monitoring the civil rights movement and was determined to prevent the emergence of a "black messiah" who would stir revolt among black Americans. King was high on his hit list. So when Hoover tied King to Levison, it was more of an attempt to tarnish King than it was concerns about Levison. Hoover would continue to try to smear King, attempting to tie him to communism and extramarital affairs. The FBI would even send King a letter urging him to commit suicide or else they would reveal his "filthy, fraudulent self" to the world. That letter would be mailed in 1964.

On June 22, Kennedy and King gathered with the other civil rights leaders in the Cabinet Room. JFK told the gathering that his poll numbers had plunged since he came out in strong support of civil rights, but that he was firmly behind the cause. When prompted to offer his reaction to the planned march, he said, "We want success in the Congress, not a big show on the Capitol."

The response indicated that Kennedy didn't like the idea of a march, but, on the other hand, he didn't demand that they prevent it. The venerable Randolph then announced, in a booming voice, "There *will* be a march." Vice President Lyndon Johnson argued that legislation was the best remedy, but King remarked that both were needed. Other civil rights group leaders said they would face opposition from their followers if they did *not* march.

Perhaps weary of the two-hour meeting, the president concluded by saying, "Well, we all have our problems. You have your problems, I have my problems." Kennedy then left to begin an important trip to Europe, where he would attempt to negotiate a nuclear test-ban treaty and to assure Western Europeans of America's commitment to defend them against Communist threats. In other words, it seems, he felt that he had bigger fish to fry.

Since the president had not attempted to squelch the March on Washington, King and Randolph continued with their plans to stage it. Meanwhile, King returned to his succession of speaking engagements, which included a speech in Detroit, Michigan, on June 23. When he arrived in the Motor City, he was amazed by the size of the gathering. Some 125,000 people, which the *Detroit Free Press* labeled "the largest civil rights demonstration in the nation's history," participated in a "Freedom Walk" down Woodward Avenue to Cobo Hall. Organized by Tony Brown and other local civil rights leaders, the theme of the march was jobs for African Americans—in automotive plants, construction, and other industries.

Inside a packed Cobo Hall, King delivered a speech that has been called the prequel to his "I Have a Dream" speech. MLK said "I have a dream" twelve times in his Detroit speech, and he used the phrase "justice will roll down like waters, and righteousness like a mighty stream." The conclusion of King's speech was similar to the famous one in Washington. He declared: "With this faith, we will be able to achieve this new day when all of God's children, black men and white men, Jews and Gentiles, Protestants and Catholics, will be able to join hands and sing with the Negroes in the spiritual of old: Free at last! Free at last! Thank God almighty, we are free at last!"

After the Detroit demonstration, United Auto Workers (UAW) president Walter Reuther hosted a meeting of the major civil rights leaders. These men, including the skeptical Roy Wilkins—the powerful head of the NAACP—showed support for the march. "We all adopted it," Wilkins wrote, "broadening its purpose to back the civil rights bill. The March on Washington was on."

The first big planning meeting occurred on July 2, 1963, at the Roosevelt Hotel in New York. When Wilkins arrived, he was frustrated to see that fifteen men had been invited to participate. For Wilkins, that was too many "chiefs." Wilkins "began literally to tap the men on the shoulders, saying 'This one stays. This one goes.' . . . Wilkins cut through the group like a scythe."

By the time Wilkins was through, six "chiefs" remained and the rest were left to grumble in the hallways. The "Big Six," as they would be called, were Wilkins (of course), King, Randolph, National Urban League Executive Director Whitney Young, CORE Executive Director James Farmer, and SNCC Chairman John Lewis.

March organizers Bayard Rustin (*left*) and Cleveland Robinson

Randolph wanted his longtime colleague Bayard Rustin to head the march, but Wilkins strongly opposed the idea. He felt that Rustin's homosexuality, past ties to communism, and antiwar stances would subject the civil rights movement to relentless attacks. "Randolph held his ground," Wilkins wrote, "so we worked out a compromise. Rustin did most of the work, but he had to stay in the background."

To appease Wilkins and Young, Randolph agreed to open the leadership of the march to whites. The Big Six would eventually expand to the "Top Ten." The four new members included Reuther, who would represent labor unions; Mathew Ahmann, the executive director of the National Catholic Conference; Reverend Eugene Carson Blake, vice chairman of the Commission on Race Relations for the National Council of Churches of Christ in America; and Rabbi Joachim Prinz, president of the American Jewish Conference.

While the organizers planned for a peaceful march, fear-mongers predicted the worst. Reported *Ebony* magazine in 1963: "ripples of fear spread across the nation. Washington, D.C., already more than one-half Negro, was hysterical; the general feeling, the *Washington Daily News* said, was that the Vandals were coming again to sack Rome. Powerful politicians and big men in labor and business urged the leaders to abandon the March. . . . The press took up the cry, saying with increasing stridence that the March was social dynamite and that violence was almost unavoidable."

As Senate hearings on the civil rights bill proceeded in July, segregationists such as Mississippi governor Ross Barnett declared that the civil rights movement was a Communist conspiracy. On July 13, a headline in the *New York Times* read "Barnett Charges Kennedys Assist Red Racial Plot." In Senate hearings, both Barnett and Alabama governor George Wallace displayed photographs of King speaking in 1957 at Highlander Folk School, which they inaccurately described as a Communist training school.

While the march and the movement were taking a lot of heat, President Kennedy spoke on their behalf in a July 17 press conference. He stated: "I think that the way that the Washington march is now developed, which is a peaceful assembly calling for a redress of grievances, the cooperation with the police, every evidence that it is going to be peaceful . . . I think that is in the great tradition. I look forward to being here. I am sure Members of Congress will be here. We want citizens to come to Washington if they feel that they are not having their rights expressed."

Despite the president's support, the opposition wouldn't let up. On August 13, fifteen days before the scheduled march, Senator Strom Thurmond of South Carolina attacked Rustin for his Communist ties, homosexuality, and refusal to serve in World War II. As soon as he could, Randolph staged a press conference in which he, surrounded by other march leaders, declared his support for Rustin. When a reporter asked if Rustin would resign, Randolph retorted, "Why, heavens no. He's Mr. March himself!"

From that point forward, the civil rights leaders had momentum on their side. The march was on.

"If I had a Hammer"

IF I HAD A HAMMER
I'D HAMMER IN THE MORNING
I'D HAMMER IN THE EVENING
ALL OVER THIS LAND
I'D HAMMER OUT DANGER
I'D HAMMER OUT A WARNING
I'D HAMMER OUT LOVE BETWEEN MY BROTHERS AND
MY SISTERS
ALL OVER THIS LAND

WELL I'VE GOT A HAMMER
AND I'VE GOT A BELL
AND I'VE GOT A SONG TO SING
ALL OVER THIS LAND
IT'S THE HAMMER OF JUSTICE
IT'S THE BELL OF FREEDOM
IT'S THE SONG ABOUT LOVE BETWEEN MY BROTHERS
AND MY SISTERS
ALL OVER THIS LAND

The words and music were originally written by folk singers Lee Hays and Pete Seeger. The trio Peter, Paul, & Mary rewrote the melody and sang their version at the 1963 march.

CHAPTER FOUR

PREPARATIONS

Planning a dinner party for ten guests can be nerve-wracking; arranging a wedding for a hundred is almost overwhelming. So imagine what Bayard Rustin was up against when he had to organize a march for 100,000 people—and had less than two months to do it.

When he began this monumental task in early July, Rustin had two other factors working against him. The Top Ten, who undoubtedly would have their own opinions about how the March on Washington should be run, were scattered across the country. Secondly, the organizing committee didn't yet have enough money to stage this massive event. To address the first problem, Rustin established a headquarters in Harlem and insisted that each of the Top Ten have a representative at that location. Raising funds was a bigger issue.

The organizers needed to pay for the printing of press releases, instructions for the marchers, and signs for them to carry. (They would ban homemade signs for fear of vulgar or hateful messages.) They also wanted to transport and house thousands of poor and unemployed people to the march, which Rustin figured would cost $15,000. All told, the budget was approximately $75,000. The NAACP, National Urban League, and the trade unions (thanks to Walter Reuther) all donated substantial sums of money and helped with bus transportation. Organizers worked to raise money and solicit the donation of supplies from other sources.

Simultaneously, organizers tried to recruit people to come to the march. Through the black media and mailing lists, organizers issued a newsletter. Typed on a manual typewriter and then mimeographed, the newsletter encouraged readers to spread the word of the march to local media and, if they could, donate funds. It also updated readers on the exciting developments to that point. "In the South," it stated, "plans are under way for a Freedom Train from Tallahassee, Florida on August 27, and will travel along the east coast to Washington, picking up people as it goes."

The newsletter noted that buses and planes had been chartered from Chicago. In Washington, "city government authorities have advised departmental heads to give their employees the day off where possible." And in New York, "at least thirty or forty thousand people will leave the city by bus, plane, and train. Mayor [Robert F.] Wagner has declared August 28 Jobs and Freedom Day. City employees have permission to take the day off, presumably with pay."

Those who wanted to attend the march had to figure out a way to finance their trip. African Americans held fund-raising parties, bake sales, and even fashion shows to raise the money for bus fare. And how would all those buses, which would number in the hundreds, navigate through the streets of Washington? Rustin had it covered. He arranged with city officials to ban street parking in a large area of the city on that day. He also insisted that each bus have a "captain," who would be given an envelope of directions and instructions. Meanwhile, the city agreed to run trains and buses to the National Mall.

The march headquarters would be in a giant green tent, filled with telephones installed by the phone company. Hundreds of pay phones would be installed throughout the area. Rustin also arranged for several thousand portable toilets, twenty-one drinking fountains, twenty-four first-aid stations, and dozens of doctors and nurses. The U.S. Army provided 40,000 blankets for those who would arrive early and sleep overnight. Rustin tried to make sure that no one would go hungry; volunteers agreed to provide beverages, sandwiches, and fruit to thirsty and famished marchers.

A variety of approved signs were produced, each with a direct message: "We Demand Equal Rights Now!;" "We March for Integrated Schools Now;" "Civil Rights Plus Full Employment Equals Freedom."

While racial idealists dreamed of a "color-blind" society, Rustin was highly conscious of color when arranging law enforcement for the march. Most of the big-city riots that would rage in the mid- to late '60s would be sparked by a racial incident between white police and black citizens. Rustin knew he had to avoid such a possibility. Thus, he organized his own force comprised of professional but non-uniformed officers. They would carry handcuffs but would not be armed. Moreover, Rustin divided his force into two units, one black and one white. Black officers would arrest only black individuals, and whites would arrest only whites. Far away from the demonstration, several thousand uniformed police officers would be on duty, and National Guardsmen would be at the ready in case violence did erupt.

A number of labor unions agreed to send representatives to the march, but to Randolph's dismay the AFL-CIO bowed out. The largest federation of unions in the United States, the AFL-CIO had millions of members. Randolph believed they said no because of internal politics; leadership did not want to alienate the many southern white members who strongly opposed the march.

On a positive note, many celebrities announced that they would join the march. African Americans such as Harry Belafonte, Sammy Davis Jr., Sidney Poitier, and Lena Horne said they were coming, as did white actors Paul Newman and Marlon Brando and white folk singers Joan Baez and Bob Dylan. To some degree, the march marked the beginning of white entertainers stepping forward as political progressives—a trend that would continue into the new century with Sean Penn, Bono, George Clooney, Susan Sarandon, and many, many others.

With so many celebrities saying they were coming, the organizing committee decided to put them to work. The organizers divided the march's program into two parts. First, the entertainers would perform in front of the Washington Monument. Then the crowd would walk 0.8 miles to the Lincoln Memorial, where civil rights leaders would speak.

Late in the organizational process, Rustin and Cleveland Robinson—chairman of the Administrative Committee—released "Final Plans for the March on Washington for Jobs and Freedom." The manual sheds insight on the details and objectives of the march. Under "What We Demand," the manual listed ten goals. They were, verbatim:

Actors Sidney Poitier (*left*), Harry Belafonte (center), and Charlton Heston

1. Comprehensive and effective *civil rights legislation* from the present Congress—without compromise or filibuster—to guarantee all Americans, access to all public accommodations, decent housing, adequate and integrated education, and the right to vote.

2. Withholding of Federal funds from all programs in which discrimination exists.

3. *Desegregation of all school districts in 1963.*

4. Enforcement of the *Fourteenth Amendment*—reducing Congressional representation of states where citizens are disfranchised.

5. A new *Executive Order* banning discrimination in all housing supported by federal funds.

6. Authority for the Attorney General to institute *injunctive suits* when any constitutional right is violated.

7. A massive federal program to train and place all unemployed workers—Negro and white—on meaningful and dignified jobs at decent wages.

8. A national *minimum wage* act that will give all Americans a decent standard of living. (Government surveys show that anything less than $2.00 an hour fails to do this.)

9. A broadened *Fair Labor Standards Act* to include all areas of employment which are presently excluded.

10. A federal *Fair Employment Practices Act* barring discrimination by federal, state and municipal governments, and by employers, contractors, employment agencies, and trade unions.

Explaining the reasons for the march, the organizers didn't mince words. "[T]he rate of Negro unemployment is nearly three times that of whites," they stated. "Their livelihoods destroyed, the Negro unemployed are thrown into the streets, driven to despair, to hatred, to crime, to violence. All America is robbed of their potential contribution."

All of the civil rights leaders were concerned that Congress would shoot down or water down the pending civil rights bill. The march organizers boldly stated: "Despite this crisis, reactionary Republicans and Southern Democrats in Congress are still working to defeat effective civil rights legislation. They fight against the rights of all workers and minority groups. They are sworn enemies of freedom and justice. They proclaim states rights in order to destroy human rights."

On the morning of August 28, civil rights leaders hoped to meet with President Kennedy. In addition, all members of Congress would be invited to the Lincoln Memorial presentation. Reserve seating would be made available to them, and the organizers promised to make public the names of those who attended. The massive march of 100,000-plus demonstrators—portraying the power of the people—would be the third prong in their lobbying effort.

As August 28 neared, African Americans became increasingly excited about the event. Organizers realized that a lot more than 100,000 people—in fact, perhaps 200,000—could be coming, including some unwelcome guests. The American Nazi Party distributed its own set of leaflets. "August 28 will be the day that the White Man will sweep away the Black Revolution, as though it never existed," a flyer stated. "Washington, D.C., will be the battle ground." The FBI monitored this hate group, and the U.S. military made sure that troops would be at the ready in the event of a major disturbance.

George Lincoln Rockwell (*center*) and members of the American Nazi Party stop to fill gas in their "hate bus" during a stop in Montgomery, Alabama, in May 1961.

Prior to the march, numerous threats were made. One person threatened to blow up the *Los Angeles Times* building unless his or her letter was published in the newspaper. The letter referred to President Kennedy as a "Nigger lover" and informed the president that "I have an offer on your life." He added, "Oll we want the Niggers stay away from whites places. If not be too many killings."

Bomb threats continued up to the day of the event. For more than a week, daily bomb threats were made at the march headquarters in New York and Washington.

Undeterred, organizers proceeded with their plans. They decided that the Lincoln Memorial program would include eighteen parts, mostly a mix of "remarks" (speeches), songs, and prayer. Each of the Top Ten would speak, but Rustin put a strict time limit on each. He warned them that a "hook man would unceremoniously yank them from the podium if their speeches exceeded seven minutes." No one questioned the selection of Martin Luther King as the final speaker, for he was universally regarded as the most dynamic orator.

Before march day, all the speakers had to submit their speeches to the organizing committee. Robert Kennedy's staff read the speeches and was concerned about the militant tone of John Lewis's. Fellow SNCC leader James Forman had added lines that equated the civil rights movement to Union General William T. Sherman's massively destructive march through Georgia during the Civil War.

"We will march through the South, through the heart of Dixie, the way Sherman did," Lewis's speech read. "We shall pursue our own 'scorched earth' policy and burn Jim Crow to the ground— nonviolently. We shall crack the South into a thousand pieces and put them back together in the image of democracy." Archbishop Patrick O'Boyle, who would begin the March on Washington program with an invocation, was among those who thought the passage was inappropriate. Lewis and civil rights leaders would go back and forth on this speech until the very last minute.

The final days before the march were incredibly tense. King and Wilkins appeared on the NBC news show *Meet the Press*, in which reporter Lawrence Spivak stated that numerous authorities "believe it would be impossible to bring more than 100,000 militant Negroes into Washington without incidents and possible rioting." The civil rights movement, at least up to 1963, was by no means "militant," but opponents of the march promulgated that myth. "You are committing the worst possible mistake in promoting this march," said Senator Olin D. Johnston of South Carolina. "You should know that criminal, fanatical, and communistic elements, as well as crackpots, will move in to take every advantage of this mob."

As march day approached, fears of violence permeated Washington. To prepare for a deluge of casualties, Washington hospitals canceled elective surgery. The city banned the sale of liquor to prevent drunken rowdiness, and the Washington Senators, a major-league baseball team, postponed two games. From his Washington headquarters (a tent near the Washington Monument), Rustin "announced that the psychology of peace was fragile and that there was no telling what might happen if attackers burned one of the two thousand buses headed toward Washington, as they had burned the Freedom Ride bus, or if any bombs were detonated, as in Birmingham."

Partly to keep marchers satisfied (i.e., peaceful), volunteers at New York's Riverside Church prepared 80,000 bag lunches for the masses. Organizers worked frantically over the last few days. According to *Time* magazine, Rustin handed out "volley after volley of handbooks, bulletins, press releases, charts, schedules, visceral warnings and soul-stirring exhortations." Organizers urged "marchers to bring plenty of water—but not 'alcoholic refreshments.' They suggested peanut butter and jelly sandwiches, emphasized the shortcomings of mayonnaise 'as it deteriorates, and may cause serious diarrhea.' They reminded everyone to wear low-heeled shoes, to bring a raincoat, to wear a hat, to remember their sunglasses."

One person who wouldn't attend the march was President Kennedy. According to historian Thomas C. Reeves in *A Question of Character: A Life of John F. Kennedy*, JFK "felt that he would be

Bayard Rustin, addressing a group of march marshals in New York as they prepare for the March on Washington

booed at the march, and also didn't want to meet with organizers before the march because he didn't want a list of demands." Instead, the president said he would meet with the Big Ten at the White House late in the afternoon, after the ceremonies were over.

Those who expected a march of "militant Negroes" were completely off the mark. Most marchers looked forward to being part of an exciting, historic event—a day to celebrate and cherish. On Tuesday, August 27, the *New York Times* reported on a six-bus caravan of African Americans who were on their way to Washington. "I guess you could call me a combination freedom rider and tourist on this trip," said twenty-year-old Willie Leonard. Henry Haynes, eighty-one, said he was most looking forward to seeing the White House. One African American woman, who worked as a maid for a white woman, said her boss gave her time off to make the trip. "She said have a good time," the woman said.

One older rider in the group was unfazed by the twenty-hour journey. "You forget we Negroes have been riding buses all our lives," he said.

On Tuesday, newspapers across the country ran stories of people heading to the march. In Florida, a "Freedom Special" locomotive roared northward pulling thirteen cars, each with accommodations for sixty people. It was expected to add cars as it chugged through Georgia, the Carolinas, and Virginia. From Chicago, two thirty-seven car trains—one of which included a jazz combo—headed for the nation's capital. Activists in Chicago, Philadelphia, New Orleans, and other cities chartered "Freedom Buses."

Some of the stories were extraordinary. Jay Hardo, an eighty-two-year-old man from Dayton, Ohio, rode his bicycle to Washington, with the image of an American eagle on his handlebars. Ledger Smith, a twenty-seven-year-old NAACP member from Chicago, roller-skated seven hundred miles to be part of history. Days before the march, African American David Parker and five of his friends motored in an old Ford from Los Angeles to Washington "because," Parker said, "my people got troubles."

Trampling on the old myth that black Americans were "lazy," members of CORE's Brooklyn chapter walked 230 miles on behalf of social justice. From Alabama, teenagers Robert Thomas, Robert Avery, and James F. Smith—all members of the Gadsden Student Movement—walked and hitchhiked seven hundred miles. Arriving a few days early, they were put to work by the organizing committee.

On August 27, the leaders of the March on Washington for Jobs and Freedom issued a statement. They insisted that the march "will be orderly, but not subservient. It will be proud, but not arrogant. It will be nonviolent, but not timid."

Thousands of demonstrators arrived either on the day before the march or in the wee hours of the morning on Wednesday the 28th. As dawn broke at approximately 6:30 a.m., anticipation filled the air.

"When [our] train pulled into Union Station," said Reverend Abraham Woods, who hailed from Florida, "we saw buses coming from everywhere filled with people. I'm telling you, we were just elated."

"A Pawn in their Game"

A BULLET FROM THE BACK OF A BUSH TOOK
MEDGAR EVERS' BLOOD.
A FINGER FIRED THE TRIGGER TO HIS NAME.
A HANDLE HID OUT IN THE DARK,
A HAND SET THE SPARK,
TWO EYES TOOK THE AIM,
BEHIND A MAN'S BRAIN;
BUT HE CAN'T BE BLAMED–
HE'S ONLY A PAWN IN THEIR GAME.

A SOUTH POLITICIAN PREACHES
TO THE POOR WHITE MAN,
"YOU GOT MORE THAN THE BLACKS,
DON'T COMPLAIN.
YOU'RE BETTER THAN THEM, YOU BEEN BORN
WITH WHITE SKIN," THEY EXPLAIN.
AND THE NEGRO'S NAME
IS USED IT IS PLAIN
FOR THE POLITICIAN'S GAIN
AS HE RISES TO FAME
AND THE POOR WHITE REMAINS
ON THE CABOOSE OF THE TRAIN
BUT IT AIN'T HIM TO BLAME
HE'S ONLY A PAWN IN THEIR GAME.

This is Bob Dylan's song about the assassination
of civil rights leader Medgar Evers. The "pawn" of
which Dylan sings is Byron De La Beckwith, the white
supremacist who shot Evers. Dylan's song exposes
the larger and more entrenched issue of racism and
prejudice in America.

CHAPTER FIVE
A QUARTER-MILLION STRONG

Jean Shepherd, the man who wrote the book *A Christmas Story* and served as narrator for the movie version, attended the March on Washington. Riding a bus from New York City, he was amazed at the sights and sounds when he entered Washington's city limits on the morning of August 28: "[We were] riding along one of the main streets through the slums and here were hundreds of people on the steps—grandmothers, little old ladies, skinny kids, nuns, tough-looking guys who worked as garage mechanics . . . everywhere they're waving, we're happy you're here."

The morning arrivals sang some of the "Freedom Songs" that were popular during the civil rights movement. Rooted in gospel music, these songs had messages that were relevant to the movement and, in particular, this special day. The titles said it all: "We Shall Overcome," "I'm on My Way," "Ain't Gon' Let Nobody Turn Me Around."

Fifteen-year-old Ericka Jenkins lived in one of those Washington slums that Shepherd mentioned. As she made her way from her world of brick and concrete to the grassy expanse of the National Mall, she too was amazed—not by the locals, but by the influx of visitors. "I've never been so awestruck," she recalled. "They came every way—flatbed trucks with the wood floor that they used to carry tobacco, pickup trucks that were all dinged up, charter buses, school buses, station wagons, cars, motorcycles, bicycles, tricycles, and I could see people still coming in groups."

Jenkins made her way to the Washington Monument, where by 9 a.m. some 40,000 people had gathered. "I saw people laughing and listening and standing very close to one another, almost in an embrace," she wrote. "Children of every size, pregnant women, elderly people who seemed tired but happy to be there, clothing that made me know that they struggled to make it day to day."

What intrigued most of the marchers was the racial mix of the crowd—approximately ten white people for every thirty black visitors. And unlike the beaches and movie theaters of the Deep South, this gathering was completely integrated. It was enough to make George Lincoln Rockwell cringe.

Founder of the American Nazi Party, which brandished the same swastika of Hitler's Nazi Party, Rockwell had planned his own march on Washington. He boasted that two hundred of his white-supremacist colleagues would join him, but only about seventy-five showed up. Police permitted his people to gather in a small grassy area, but they did not have a permit to speak. Rockwell's deputy chief, Karl R. Allen, spoke anyway: "We are here to protest in a peaceful manner the occupation of the nation's capital with people deadly to the welfare of the country." When Allen continued to talk despite warnings not to, he was arrested. It was the first arrest of the day.

By 11 a.m., the crowd had swollen to nearly 100,000. Weather forecasters had predicted a humid afternoon, with temperatures in the mid-eighties—typical for Washington in late August. Thousands of demonstrators wore the "March on Washington"

George Lincoln Rockwell, self-styled leader of the American Nazi Party, puffs on a corncob pipe as he poses at the Washington Monument, on August 28, 1963.

buttons that the organizing committee had sold to help fund the event. For fifty cents each, many people purchased the cheese-sandwich bag lunches that church volunteers had packed. Others opted for the hot dogs, ice cream, and soft drinks that vendors were hawking. As more and more people arrived, lines for drinking fountains and the portable toilets got longer and longer.

The mass influx of visitors did not please everyone in the city. *New York Times* columnist James Reston opined that residents in the white enclave of northwest Washington were annoyed by the intrusion. Their bars were closed, he wrote, and they couldn't "get a taxi downtown, or count on the colored cook coming in for dinner."

Back on the National Mall, singers and other celebrities kept the crowd from growing restless. Shortly after 10 a.m., folksinger Joan Baez got the ball rolling with "Oh Freedom." Odetta and Josh White, black singers and civil rights activists, performed next, followed by the trio of Peter, Paul & Mary. They sang their new hit song "Blowin' in the Wind," a Bob Dylan original that was becoming an anthem of the 1960s. The song includes the following lines:

> Yes, how many years can some people exist
> Before they're allowed to be free?
> Yes, how many times can a man turn his head
> Pretending he just doesn't see?
> The answer my friend is blowin' in the wind
> The answer is blowin' in the wind.

Dylan himself took the stage, performing a song he had recently written about the murder of activist Medgar Evers. Black comedian Dick Gregory and actor Burt Lancaster were among those who spoke to the crowd. For some of the poor, rural visitors, this was the first time they ever saw celebrities. One can imagine their joy in seeing the legendary Jackie Robinson, the courageous hero who had broken Major League Baseball's color barrier in 1947 and went on to become the National League's Most Valuable Player. Robinson was there with one of his sons.

Folk singers Joan Baez
and Bob Dylan

Hazel Mangle Rivers, a black woman who had made the trip from Alabama, was impressed with the civility of the large, racially mixed crowd. "The people are lots better up here than they are down South," she said. "They treat you much nicer. Why, when I was out there at the march a white man stepped on my foot, and he said, 'Excuse me,' and I said 'Certainly!' That's the first time that has ever happened to me. I believe that was the first time a white person has ever really been nice to me."

At 11:30, the Top Ten were scheduled to lead the march from the Washington Monument to the Lincoln Memorial. However, the leaders were still at the Capitol, meeting with members of Congress. Knowing exactly where to go and wanting to get good seats, marchers headed in that direction—sans their leaders. Many sang Freedom Songs as they marched down Constitution and Independence avenues.

"My God, they're *going*!" Rustin shouted from the steps of the Capitol. "We're supposed to be leading *them*!" The Top Ten were hustled toward the stream of marchers. The ten men held hands and gave the impression that they were leading the people, even though they were somewhere in the middle.

Demonstrators sit, with their feet in the Reflecting Pool at the Lincoln Memorial, during the March on Washington.

By this point, the crowd had swelled to some 200,000, yet police were impressed by their behavior. When a young man disrupted the march by tearing someone's placard, he became just the third and final arrest of the day—which hardly constituted the "riot" that cynics had predicted. Before the day was over, several dozen people would be sent by ambulance to a hospital for heat exhaustion, but only four would be admitted. No deaths were recorded at the march.

As the massive crowd moved toward the Lincoln Memorial, the event took on a different feel. Hundreds stopped and sat on the edge of the giant Reflecting Pool, where they cooled their feet in the water. The image of blacks and whites pressed next to each other, their bare feet in the pool, was certainly unique. In the long history of Jim Crow, seemingly everything associated with water had been strictly segregated. Many whites feared that blacks would somehow contaminate the water, so swimming pools, beaches, drinking fountains, and outhouses could not be shared by the races.

To illustrate: When black protesters used the pool at the Monson Motor Lodge in St. Augustine, Florida, in June 1964, the motel manager poured hydrochloric acid into the water in an effort to force them out. A week later, a club-wielding police force ran into the Gulf of Mexico to beat black activists who were trying to desegregate the beach. But on August 28, blacks and whites shared the Reflecting Pool in harmony and without incident.

As the start of the program neared (it would begin after 1:30), the drama began to intensify. CBS covered the march live, bringing the historic, unprecedented event into millions of homes. Due to new satellite technology, the event was broadcast live in Europe, where the British, French, and others saw an aspect of America that they had never seen before. In London, Paris, and other cities, people staged their own demonstrations in support of the march.

At one point before the program began, Roy Wilkins announced over the loudspeakers that ninety-five-year-old W. E. B. Du Bois had died the previous day. The announcement added a somber significance to the day, for Du Bois—a co-founder of the NAACP—had been one of the leading civil rights voices in the first half of the twentieth century.

As the start time neared, Rustin's carefully planned program was in jeopardy—not due to disruptions in the crowd but because of the egos among his ranks. A small brushfire involved Birmingham activist Reverend Fred Shuttlesworth, who was still upset that he was not allowed to speak. But of bigger concern was the issue over John Lewis's speech, which had not been resolved. The latest draft, cried Walter Reuther and others, was still much too harsh. Archbishop Patrick O'Boyle threatened to walk off the podium if the speech was delivered as written—a real problem since O'Boyle was scheduled to open the program with an invocation.

Assistant Attorney General Burke Marshall arrived at the Lincoln Memorial in the sidecar of a motorcycle carrying a revised version of the speech. Needless to say, that did not go over well with Lewis. The backstage arguments over the speech were so loud that Rustin ordered the playing of the National Anthem on the loudspeakers to drown out the squabbling. Lewis and Wilkins were shaking fingers in each other's faces when Rustin appointed King, Randolph, and Eugene Carson Blake to sit down with Lewis and reach a compromise on the speech—pronto.

Stalling for time, Rustin sent several esteemed individuals to the podium to make brief remarks, including Shuttlesworth. Meanwhile, in a room underneath the giant seat of the Lincoln Memorial, the temperamental Lewis was bowing to the will of the man he had long idolized, Martin Luther King. The "scorched earth" language was still in the speech, and Randolph, Blake, and King believed it was time for it to go. "John, I know you as well as anybody," King said. "That doesn't *sound* like you." Lewis allowed King to handwrite some changes, which James Forman made on a portable typewriter. The crisis was averted—finally.

March organizers gather at the Lincoln Memorial. (*From left to right*) Mathew Ahmann, executive director of the National Catholic Conference for Interracial Justice; (*seated with glasses*) Cleveland Robinson, chairman of the demonstration committee; (*beside Robinson*) A. Philip Randolph, organizer of the demonstration and veteran labor leader; (*standing behind the two chairs*) Rabbi Joachim Prinz, president of the American Jewish Congress; (*wearing a bow tie and standing beside Prinz*) Joseph Rauh, Jr., a Washington, D.C. attorney and civil rights, peace, and union activist; John Lewis, chairman of the Student Nonviolent Coordinating Committee; and Floyd McKissick, national chairman of the Congress of Racial Equality.

Outside, participants in the program sat on a platform that was constructed on the steps of the Lincoln Memorial. Looking straight ahead, they saw an expanse of land that can be compared to a giant football field. Trees lined the "sidelines" for eight-tenths of a mile, and at the far end the Washington Monument served as the "end zone." Immediately in front of the platform were rows of chairs set up for members of Congress. A ways behind the chairs was the enormous, horizontal Reflecting Pool. The marchers filled in the remaining area between the Lincoln Memorial and Washington Monument, and they also spilled out to the sides of the Memorial.

To the people who had fulfilled his decades-long dream of a march on Washington, Randolph delivered the opening remarks. A former Shakespearean actor, Randolph spoke with a deep baritone voice. "Fellow Americans," he boomed, "we are gathered here in the largest demonstration in the history of this nation. . . . [Our purpose is] to let the nation and world know the meaning of our numbers. We are not a pressure group. We are not an organization or a group of organizations. We are not a mob. We are the advance guard of a massive, moral revolution for jobs and freedom."

Except for the Eva Jessye Choir and gospel singer Mahalia Jackson, "entertainment" would not be provided during the program. The speakers knew that they themselves needed to be the entertainment. Their words needed to sing and dance, to inspire the people and touch them emotionally. Randolph knew how to move a crowd, and he did so with the concluding words of his speech: "When we leave it will be to carry the civil rights movement home with us, into every nook and cranny of the land. And we shall return again and again to Washington in ever-growing numbers until total freedom is ours."

After Randolph, Eugene Carson Blake, the former president of the National Council of Churches, took the podium. Blake, a Presbyterian, was proactive on civil rights issues. Just a month earlier, he was among the 283 people arrested in Maryland for demonstrating at a segregated amusement park.

Blake addressed the crowd: "Yes, we come to march behind and with these amazingly able leaders of the Negro American who, to the shame of almost every white American, have alone and without us mirrored the suffering of the cross of Jesus Christ. They have offered their bodies to arrest and violence, to the hurt and indignity of fire hoses and dogs, of derisions and of poverty and some death for this just cause."

Throughout the 1960s, African American women would criticize the movement as being patriarchal—ruled and dominated by men. No women comprised the Top Ten, and none were scheduled to speak during the program. After Blake's remarks, however, Randolph stepped to the podium with several women in what was officially called "Tribute to Negro Women Fighters for Freedom."

Myrlie Evers was supposed to be one of the honored women, but transportation problems prevented her from being there. Evers had been at home two months earlier when her husband, NAACP Field Secretary Medgar Evers, was fatally shot on their driveway for protesting segregation. She would one day become the chairwoman of the NAACP. Prince Lee had endured the death of her husband, Herbert Lee, a farmer from McComb, Mississippi, who had been shot for trying to help black citizens register to vote.

Also honored were Rosa Parks, the hero of the Montgomery bus boycott, and Daisy Bates, who had played a leading role in helping nine black students integrate Little Rock Central High School in 1957. The crowd also applauded the heroics of Diane Nash, a Freedom Rider and co-founder of the SNCC who had also helped lead a massive desegregation movement in Nashville, Tennessee. (With TV cameras rolling, Nash had brazenly asked the Nashville mayor if he thought racial discrimination was wrong, and he admitted that he did.) Gloria Richardson was the sixth woman honored. She was the bold leader of the Cambridge Nonviolent Action Committee, which used the power of protest to eradicate segregation in that city.

John Lewis spoke next. The son of Alabama sharecroppers, Lewis had defied all odds to earn a degree from Fisk University. With the SNCC, he had participated in sit-ins as well as the 1961 Freedom Rides, in which he suffered beatings by whites in Rock Hill, South Carolina, and Montgomery, Alabama. Just twenty-three, Lewis was part of a younger, more demanding faction of the movement. Veterans such as Randolph, Wilkins, and King had nudged open the door of racial oppression a millimeter at a time; young guns like Lewis were anxious to bash the whole door down.

Besides the "scorched earth" language of his original speech, Lewis had included the following sentence: "In good conscience, we cannot support wholeheartedly the administration's civil rights bill, for it is too little and too late." That line was eliminated, for it was poor PR to badmouth the most important civil rights bill in almost a hundred years. Another excised sentence was: "The black masses are on the march for jobs and freedom, and we must say to the politicians that there won't be a 'cooling-off' period." The Kennedy administration and civil rights leaders knew that such a

I WAS THERE

MEMORIAL

MA
FOR JU
AUGU

SPE
POLICE
D C

Twelve-year-old
Edith Lee-Payne
of Detroit,
Michigan

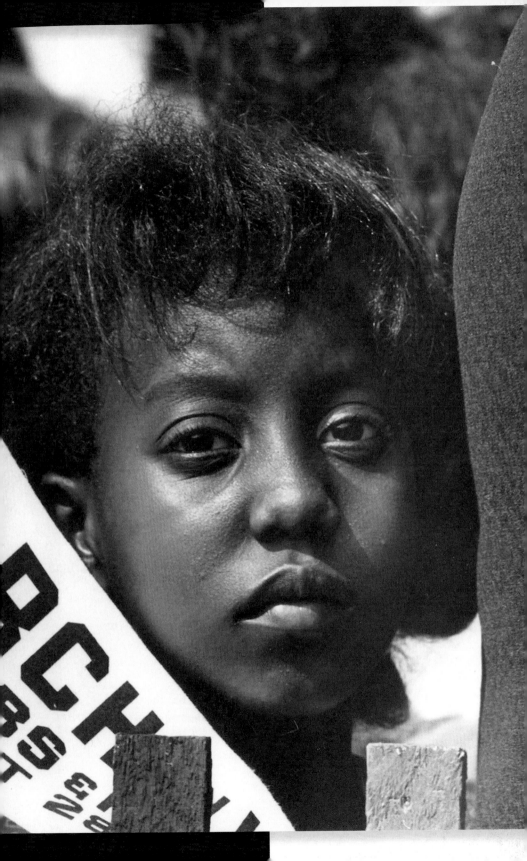

"threat" could lead to significant backlash from opponents of the movement. Forty years later, a wiser Lewis admitted that he and fellow SNCC members "got sort of carried away" when writing the speech.

In his memoir *Walking with the Wind*, Lewis stated that his speech had not been compromised. "The speech still had fire," he wrote. "It still had bite, certainly more teeth than any other speech made that day. It still had an edge, with no talk of 'Negroes'—I spoke instead of 'black citizens' and 'the black masses,' the only speaker that day to use those terms."

When he reached the podium, Lewis was so nervous that he was afraid he wouldn't be able to speak. "[When I] looked out at that sea of faces, I felt a combination of great humility and incredible fear," he wrote. "I could feel myself trembling a little bit." When he spotted a contingent of fellow SNCC members cheering him on, Lewis calmed down. He then delivered a speech that was pointed and forceful.

Lewis focused largely on what needed to be included in the civil rights bill. "We must have legislation that will protect the Mississippi sharecroppers, who have been forced to leave their homes because they dared to exercise their right to register to vote," he said. "We need a bill that will provide for the homeless and starving people of this nation. We need a bill that will ensure the equality of a maid who earns five dollars a week in the home of a family whose total income is 100,000 dollars a year."

Lewis' strongest words resonated with King's "Letter From a Birmingham Jail." "To those who have said, 'Be patient and wait,' we must say that we cannot be patient," Lewis declared. "We do not want our freedom gradually but we want to be free now. We are tired. We are tired of being beat by policemen. We are tired of seeing our people locked up in jail over and over again, and then you holler 'Be patient.' How long can we be patient? We want our freedom and we want it now."

After hours of tension and anxiety, Lewis could breathe easier after concluding his speech. "As I stepped away from the podium, every black hand on the platform reached out to shake mine," he recalled. "Now, finally, for the first time that day, I was able to take my seat and soak in the spectacular scene."

Crowds surround the Reflecting Pool during the March on Washington.

Walter Reuther, the head of the United Auto Workers, spoke next. Reuther could relate to the black activists who had endured hardships in fighting for their people. As a young labor leader who had challenged the automakers in the 1930s and '40s, Reuther was beaten multiple times and survived two assassination attempts. A socialist at heart, he believed in "fair employment" and "full employment" for *all* American workers.

"To me, the civil rights question is a moral question," Reuther said. "It transcends partisan politics. And this rally today is the first step in a total effort to mobilize the moral conscience of America and to ask the people in Congress of both parties to rise above their partisan differences and enact civil rights legislation now."

James Farmer, national director of CORE, was scheduled to talk next, but he was in jail in Louisiana. Actually, he was lucky to be alive. Because Farmer had tried to organize protests in the town of Plaquemine, Louisiana, state troopers—armed with guns, tear gas, and cattle prods—went door to door looking for him. "I was meant to die that night," Farmer recalled. "They were kicking open doors, beating up blacks in the streets, interrogating them with electric cattle prods." To get out of town, Farmer laid in the back of a hearse while the driver crept along the back roads. On August 28, Farmer was back in Plaquemine and behind bars for "disturbing the peace."

Floyd B. McKissick, CORE's national chairman, read a letter from Farmer: "From a South Louisiana parish jail, I salute the March on Washington for Jobs and Freedom. Two hundred thirty-two freedom fighters jailed with me in Plaquemine, Louisiana, also send their greetings." Farmer reminded the activists that they were "at the center of the world's stage. Play well your roles in your struggle for freedom."

"Some of us may die," he wrote, "like William L. Moore or Medgar Evers, but our war is for life not for death, and we will not stop our demands for freedom now. We will not slow down. We will not stop our militant, peaceful demonstrations. . . . We will not stop till the dogs stop biting us in the South and the rats stop biting us in the North."

After Farmer's remarks, the crowd—now growing weary in the warm, humid midafternoon—welcomed a change of pace. Eva Jessye's choir, chosen by Martin Luther King for the event, performed on stage. Rabbi Uri Miller, president of the Synagogue Council of America, followed with a prayer.

Whitney Young, executive director of the National Urban League, spoke of the problems facing blacks in the ghettos. He talked about how black newborns "die three times sooner and our parents die seven years earlier." He talked of "congested, ill-equipped schools which breed dropouts and which smother motivation." But Young could not capture the crowd; not once was his speech interrupted by applause.

The sun and humidity were taking their toll on the marchers. Many tried to squeeze under the big, shady trees that bordered the area, while others jumped into the shallow Reflecting Pool. Mathew Ahmann, executive director of the National Catholic Conference for Interracial Justice, could not rouse the people. His speech lacked color and was filled with long, abstract sentences.

Roy Wilkins of the NAACP followed Ahmann. Despite a mild-mannered personality, Wilkins delivered a speech that was, at times, vividly worded. "It is simply incomprehensible . . . that the U.S. government—which can regulate the contents of a pill— apparently is powerless to prevent the physical abuse of citizens within its own borders," he said.

Regarding the pending civil rights bill, Wilkins warned: "Now the president's proposal represents so moderate an approach that if it is weakened or eliminated the remainder will be little more than sugar water. Indeed, as it stands today, the package needs strengthening, and the president should join us in fighting to be sure that we get something more than pap."

At this point, the program was actually running ahead of schedule, but the crowd was wilting in the summer sun. The weatherman who had called for a high of eighty-four degrees was wrong. By noon, it was eighty-seven. The air was thick with humidity and, undoubtedly, body odor. Few had showered since at least the day before, and now people were dripping with perspiration. At least 250,000 people attended the march (some estimates were as high as 300,000), but by this point many had left.

Then came gospel singer Mahalia Jackson, who proceeded to rejuvenate the gathering with her booming renditions of "How I Got Over" and "I Been 'Buked and I Been Scorned" (at the request of King). Blacks and whites, standing side by side, clapped in rhythm. "People fumbled for handkerchiefs," Branch recorded, "and responsive cries chased the echoes of her *a cappella* voice through the cavernous outdoors." Reporter Lerone Bennett wrote that "button-down men in front and the old women in back came to their feet screaming and shouting. . . . From different places, in different ways, with different dreams, they had come and now, hearing this sung, they were one."

Rabbi Joachim Prinz, president of the American Jewish Congress, followed Jackson on the podium. "I wish I could sing!" he quipped. He then delivered a short but poignant speech:

> When I was the rabbi of the Jewish community in Berlin under the Hitler regime, I learned many things. The most important thing that I learned under those tragic circumstances was that bigotry and hatred are not the most urgent problem. The most urgent, the most disgraceful, the most shameful, and the most tragic problem is silence.

For the 250,000 people in attendance, Prinz's words hit hard. For a hundred years after the Emancipation Proclamation, the nation had watched in virtual silence as white segregationists oppressed black Americans through separation, denial of basic rights, intimidation, and violence. Prinz continued:

> America must not become a nation of onlookers. America must not remain silent. Not merely black America, but all of America. It must speak up and act, from the president down to the humblest of us, and not for the sake of the Negro, not for the sake of the black community, but for the sake of the image, the dream, the idea, and the aspiration of America itself.

After the sobering remarks of Rabbi Prinz, the crowd was emotionally primed for the next (and last) scheduled speaker. From the programs in their hands, people knew it would be King, and they began to chant his name. ABC and NBC cut away from their afternoon programming to cover King's speech live.

Millions of people who had no intention of watching the March on Washington found themselves immersed in the moment. Many who previously had shown no interest in the civil rights movement were about to be converted. They included many of the nation's children, who were still on summer vacation and had the opportunity to watch the afternoon program. Though most men and many women were at work at the time, many stay-at-home mothers and senior citizens were about to witness the historic speech. If a black barbershop, restaurant, or other business had a TV, it undoubtedly was tuned in to this extraordinary event.

After Randolph's introduction, in which he called King "the moral leader of our nation," MLK—dressed in a dark suit and tie with a white shirt—stepped to the podium. The crowd showered him with applause. Near the front of the podium, an unexpected chant arose: "Hip, hip . . . hooray! Hip, hip . . . Hooray!" Some smiled and laughed, but the chant continued—Hip, hip . . . hooray!—ten times in all. "The next president of the United States!" someone shouted.

The ovation, which lasted a full minute, inspired the speaker. King thanked the crowd, and soon they fell silent. Due to the magnitude of the event and King's oratory skills, many sensed that they were about to witness a speech of historic significance. In fact, they were just moments away from what many historians call the greatest speech in American history.

Children near the
Washington Monument

"WE SHALL OVERCOME"

WE SHALL OVERCOME, WE SHALL OVERCOME
WE SHALL OVERCOME SOMEDAY
OH-O DEEP IN MY HEART
I DO BELIEVE
WE SHALL OVERCOME SOMEDAY
WE SHALL ALL BE FREE
WE SHALL ALL BE FREE
WE SHALL ALL BE FREE SOMEDAY
OH-O DEEP IN MY HEART
I DO BELIEVE
WE SHALL OVERCOME SOMEDAY
BLACK AND WHITE TOGETHER
BLACK AND WHITE TOGETHER
BLACK AND WHITE TOGETHER SOMEDAY
OH-O DEEP IN MY HEART
I DO BELIEVE
WE SHALL OVERCOME SOMEDAY

"We Shall Overcome" is based on the gospel song "I'll Overcome Someday," composed by an African American Methodist minister, Charles Albert Tindley. Folk singer Pete Seeger changed the "I'll" to "We Shall," and the song became an inspirational anthem of the civil rights movement. Twenty-two-year-old folk singer Joan Baez led ralliers in singing the song at the 1963 March on Washington. Civil rights movements around the world—in Bangladesh, Czechoslovakia, Northern Ireland, and South Africa, among others—have since adapted "We Shall Overcome." In 2009, Joan Baez recorded a version for protesters in Iran, with some verses in Farsi. It has also been translated into Bengali, Hindi, and Malayalam.

CHAPTER SIX

"FREE AT LAST!
FREE AT LAST!"

From the Lincoln Memorial to the Washington Monument, marchers craned their necks to catch a glimpse of the speaker. On living room couches across the country, viewers leaned forward with keen intent. Martin Luther King had been a towering figure in American society since 1955, but for the great majority of Americans, this was the first time they had seen him deliver a full speech.

With the content of his message and his powerful delivery, King commanded their full attention. The Baptist preacher spoke slowly in a deep, baritone voice, emphasizing certain words and holding out others. His first sentence set the tone: "*I* am happy . . . to *join* with you todayyyy . . . innnn what will go down in historyyyy . . . as the greatest demonstration for freedom in the *history* of our nation."

Though known as the "I Have a Dream" speech, King did not speak of his dream until the final 620 words of his 1,671-word oration. But the first thousand or so words were brilliant in their own right.

After his opening sentence, King referenced Abraham Lincoln, saying that the former president had given hope to millions of slaves by signing the Emancipation Proclamation. But a century later, he said, black Americans were still not free. In this discussion, King began the use of two techniques to great advantage: repetition and metaphor. He began three straight sentences with "One hundred years later," which gave the speech a certain structure and rhythm. He completed each of the three sentences with a descriptive metaphor. For example: "One hundred years later, the Negro lives on a lonely island of poverty in the midst of a vast ocean of material prosperity."

The context of the next two paragraphs was a metaphor in itself. The U.S. Constitution, King said, was meant to be a promissory note to all Americans— one that promised life, liberty, and the pursuit of happiness. But, he said, "America has given the Negro people a bad check, a check which has come back marked 'insufficient funds.'"

Throughout the speech, people near the podium interjected with robust applause and such call-outs as "Right on!" and "Yes!" and "Sure 'nough!" They did so when he emphasized the need to end injustice not later but *now* (like he had in "Letter From a Birmingham Jail").

Reflecting the aggressive faction of the movement— from impatient nonviolent proponent John Lewis to "by any means necessary" advocate Malcolm X—King delivered a warning to the establishment: "And those who hope that the Negro needed to blow off steam and will now be content will have a rude awakening if the nation returns to business as usual." But quickly, he reminded his fellow activists to demonstrate with dignity and discipline. "Let us not seek to satisfy our thirst for freedom by drinking from the cup of bitterness and hatred," he said.

Reverend Martin Luther King Jr. speaking

Crowd of marchers seated at the Lincoln Memorial

Next, King returned to repetition and metaphor. Six times he said that Negroes would not "be satisfied" until a specific need was met. He concluded with a paraphrasing of a biblical passage: "we will not be satisfied until 'justice rolls down like waters, and righteousness like a mighty stream.'"

After strong applause, King offered recognition to those who had gone to jail for justice. This 119-word discussion prompted little reaction from the crowd, except for polite applause at the end. That is when he transitioned from the prepared text to his off-the-cuff "I have a dream" remarks. The transition was abrupt: "I say to you today, my friends. And so even though we face the difficulties of today and tomorrow, I still have a dream."

Again using repetition, King said "I have a dream" eight times, often following with metaphorical phrases. It is here where he delivered the most memorable passage of his speech.

> I have a dream that one day on the red hills of Georgia, the sons of former slaves and the sons of former slave owners will be able to sit down together at the table of brotherhood. I have a dream that one day even the state of Mississippi, a state sweltering with the heat of injustice, sweltering with the heat of oppression, will be transformed into an oasis of freedom and justice.

Looking to the sky and then shaking his head, King bellowed to the crowd:

> I have a dream that my four little children will one day live in a nation where they will not be judged by the color of their skin but by the content of their character. I have a *dream* today!

King followed with three lines from the patriotic American song "My Country, 'Tis of Thee."

My country 'tis of thee, sweet land of liberty, of thee I sing. Land where my fathers died, land of the Pilgrim's pride. From every mountainside, let freedom ring!

King took those last three words, *let freedom ring*, and used them in nine consecutive sentences, each time almost singing the word *ring*. "Let freedom ring from Stone Mountain of Georgia . . . ," he declared, referring to the site where the Ku Klux Klan had been founded. "Let freedom ring from every hill and molehill of Mississippi." He continued, raising his right arm for emphasis, "From *every mountain*side, let freedom ring."

As the crowd roared its approval, King built up to the finale. He bellowed from the top of his lungs. He raised his arms with clenched fists. At one point, he raised up on his toes. And with his final words, he waved his right hand over the crowd, as if to bless the congregation. By letting freedom ring, King concluded,

". . . we will be able to speed up that day when all of God's children, black men and white men, Jews and Gentiles, Protestants and Catholics, will be able to join hands and sing in the words of the old Negro spiritual: Free at last! Free at last! Thank God Almighty, we are free at last!"

TIMELINE

June 25, 1941
In response to a threat of a march on Washington by black labor leader A. Philip Randolph, President Franklin Roosevelt bans racial discrimination in the defense industry.

December 5, 1955
Reverend Martin Luther King Jr. is named president of the Montgomery Improvement Association and thus will oversee the city's 381-day bus boycott.

May 17, 1957
In front of the Lincoln Memorial in Washington, D.C., King addresses 25,000 supporters at the Prayer Pilgrimage.

February 1, 1960
In Greensboro, North Carolina, four black college students stage a sit-in at a segregated lunch counter, sparking a racially mixed sit-in movement that will sweep the country.

May 2, 1963
Two weeks after King writes his "Letter From a Birmingham Jail," Birmingham officials unleash attack dogs and fire hoses on juvenile black marchers, sparking outrage across the country.

May 30, 1963
In a private phone call, King tells colleague Stanley Levison that it is time for a "mass march" on Washington.

June 19, 1963
President Kennedy strongly urges Congress to enact a civil rights act.

June 20, 1963
King announces that a march on Washington is forthcoming.

June 21, 1963
Randolph colleague Cleveland Robinson tells the press that plans are in the works for a march on Washington.

June 22, 1963

King and other civil rights leaders meet with the president about the march. Kennedy does not want it to happen, but he does not stop it.

June 23, 1963

An estimated 125,000 people participate in a "Freedom Walk" in Detroit. King delivers an initial version of his "I Have a Dream" speech inside Cobo Hall.

July 2, 1963

The first big planning meeting for the March on Washington is held at the Roosevelt Hotel in New York City. The "Big Six" leaders of the march are chosen. Bayard Rustin will organize the massive event.

July 17, 1963

President Kennedy tells the media that he looks forward to the March on Washington.

August 27, 1963

From all corners of America, citizens take such transportation as "Freedom Buses," trains, and cars to the March on Washington for Jobs and Freedom.

August 28, 1963

On a warm, humid morning, tens of thousands of marchers gather near the Washington Monument. Musical artists and other celebrities entertain the crowd.

Around midday, marchers head to the Lincoln Memorial, where the formal program will begin.

The start of the program is put in jeopardy due to the contentious rewriting of John Lewis' speech.

A. Philip Randolph is the opening speaker, and he is followed by Eugene Carson Blake. Next comes a Tribute to Negro Women Fighters for Freedom.

John Lewis follows with a toned-down but still assertive speech. Next on the podium are Walter Reuther, James Farmer, the Eva Jessye Choir, Uri Miller, Whitney Young, Mathew Ahmann, Roy Wilkins, singer Mahalia Jackson, and Joachim Prinz.

Martin Luther King delivers his "I Have a Dream" speech amid raucous applause.

SOURCES

CHAPTER 1
Growing Up with Jim Crow

p. 11,   "I'll be happy . . ." Martin Luther King Jr., *Stride Toward Freedom: The Montgomery Story* (Boston: Beacon Press, 2010), 6.

p. 11,   "Sorry, but you'll . . ." Ibid.

p. 11,   "I still remember . . ." Ibid.

p. 14,   "No jobs for . . ." Clayborne Carson, primary consultant, *Civil Rights Chronicle: The African-American Struggle for Freedom* (Lincolnwood, Ill.: Legacy Publishing, 2003), 67.

p. 15,   "A community is . . ." Manning Marable and Leith Mullings, *Let Nobody Turn Us Around* (Lanham, Md.: Rowman and Littlefield, 2009), 313.

p. 18,   "[T]he whole scene . . ." "The Bonus Army," Eyewitness to History.com, http://www.eyewitnesstohistory.com/snprelief4.htm.

p. 19,   "I'm going to . . ." William Bradford Huie, to Dan Mich, October 17, 1955, page 1, in Huie Papers at Ohio State University.

p. 19,   "So much of . . ." "The Dimensions of a Complete Life," The Martin Luther King, Jr. Research and Education Institute, http://mlk-kpp01.stanford.edu/index.php/encyclopedia/documentsentry/the_dimensions_of_a_complete_life_sermon_at_dexter_avenue_baptist_church.

CHAPTER 2
The Fight for Civil Rights

p. 21,   "I was in . . ." James M. Washington, ed., *A Testament of Hope: The Essential Writings and Speeches of Martin Luther King, Jr.* (New York: HarperCollins, 1991), 430.

p. 22,   "You know, my . . ." Andrew P. Napolitano, *Dred Scott's Revenge: A Legal History of Race and Freedom in America* (Nashville: Thomas Nelson, 2009), 183.

p. 23,   "Give us the . . ." "Give Us the Ballot," The Martin Luther King, Jr. Research and Education Institute, http://mlk-kpp01.stanford.edu/index.php/kingpapers/article/give_us_the_ballot_address_at_the_prayer_pilgrimage_for_freedom/.

p. 27,   "the torch has . . ." "John F. Kennedy: Inaugural Address," AmericanRhetoric, http://www.americanrhetoric.com/speeches/jfkinaugural.htm.

p. 27,   "Don't stop now . . ." Howard Zinn, *SNCC: The New Abolitionists* (Boston: Beacon Press, 1964), 131

p. 30,   "I've been thrown . . ." Carson, *Civil Rights Chronicle*, 211.

p. 30,   "Mississippi and her . . ." "Radio and Television Report to the Nation on the Situation at the University of Mississippi, September 30, 1962," John F. Kennedy Presidential Library and Museum, http://www.jfklibrary.org/Research/Ready-Reference/JFK-Speeches/Radio-and-Television-Report-to-the-Nation-on-the-Situation-at-the-University-of-Mississippi.aspx.

p. 31,   "Segregation now, segregation . . ." Debbie Elliott, "Wallace in the Schoolhouse Door," NPR, June 11, 2003, http://www.npr.org/2003/06/11/1294680/wallace-in-the-schoolhouse-door.

CHAPTER 3
"There *Will* Be a March"

p. 34,   "unwise and untimely . . ." Carson, *Civil Rights Chronicle*, 222.

p. 35,   "honest and open . . ." "A Call for Unity," http://en.academic.ru/dic.nsf/enwiki/870259.

p. 35,   "after more than . . ." "Letter From A Birmingham Jail," *Crisis*, November 1982, 29.

p. 35,   "when you suddenly . . ." Ibid.

p. 36,   "All you got . . ." Carson, *Civil Rights Chronicle*, 228.

p. 36,   "In spite of the . . ." Jonathan Rieder, *The Word of the Lord Is Upon Me: The Righteous Performance of Martin Luther King, Jr.* (Boston: Harvard University Press, 2008), 203.

p. 36,   "I've never forgotten . . ." Gloria Xifaras Clark, interview with Wilbur Colum, Mississippi Oral History Program, McCain Library and Archives.

p. 37,   "we are on . . ." Taylor Branch, *Parting the Waters: America in the King Years, 1954-63* (New York: Simon and Schuster, 1988), 816–817.

p. 37,   "something dramatic must . . ." Taylor Branch, *Parting the Waters*, 820.

p. 38,   "ought to be . . ." "John F. Kennedy: The American Promise to African Americans," Encyclopedia Britannica, http://www.britannica.com/presidents/article-9116924.

p. 39,   "The Negro baby . . ." Ibid.

p. 39,   "We preach freedom . . ." Ibid.

p. 40,   "told the President . . ." Branch, *Parting the Waters*, 828.

p. 42,	"In this year . . ." E. W. Kenworthy, "Civil Rights Bill Passed, 73–27," *New York Times*, June 19, 1963, http://www.nytimes.com/learning/general/onthisday/big/0619.html#article.
p. 43,	"If they shoot . . ." Branch, *Parting the Waters*, 838.
p. 44,	"filthy, fraudulent self . . ." Nick Kotz, *Judgment Days: Lyndon Baines Johnson, Martin Luther King, Jr., and the Laws that Changed America* (Boston: Houghton Mifflin, 2005), 247.
p. 44,	"We want success . . ." Ibid., 840.
p. 44,	"There *will* be . . ." Ibid.
p. 44,	"Well, we all . . ." Ibid.
p. 45,	"the largest civil . . ." Joe Darden, et al., *Detroit: Race and Uneven Development* (Philadelphia: Temple University Press, 1990), 134.
p. 45,	"I have a . . ." "Speech at the Great March on Detroit," The Martin Luther King, Jr. Research and Education Institute, http://mlk-kpp01.stanford.edu/index.php/encyclopedia/documentsentry/doc_speech_at_the_great_march_on_detroit/.
p. 45,	"We all adopted . . ." Roy Wilkins with Tom Mathews, *Standing Fast: The Autobiography of Roy Wilkins* (Cambridge, Mass.: Da Capo Press, 1994), 292.
p. 45,	"began literally to . . ." Branch, *Parting the Waters*, 847.
p. 46,	"Randolph held his . . ." Wilkins, *Standing Fast*, 292.
p. 47,	"ripples of fear . . ." Lerone Bennett, Jr., "Masses Were March Heroes," *Ebony*, November 1963.
p. 47,	"Barnett Charges Kennedys . . ." David J. Garrow, *Bearing the Cross: Martin Luther King, Jr., and the Southern Christian Leadership Conference* (New York: HarperCollins, 2004), 278.

p. 47,   "I think that . . ." "News Conference 58," John F. Kennedy Presidential Library and Museum, http://www.jfklibrary.org/Research/Ready-Reference/Press-Conferences/News-Conference-58.aspx.

p. 47,   "Why, heavens no . . ." Charles Euchner, *Nobody Turn Me Around: A People's History of the 1963 March on Washington* (Boston: Beacon Press, 2010), 116.

CHAPTER 4
Preparations

p. 50,   "In the South . . ." *March on Washington for Jobs and Freedom,* Newsletter #2, 6.

p. 50,   "city government authorities . . ." Ibid.

p. 53.   "1. Comprehensive and . . ." "What We Demand," *March on Washington for Jobs and Freedom* (newsletter), 3.

p. 54,   "[T]he rate of . . ." "Reasons for the March," *Crisis,* October 1963, 459.

p. 54,   "Despite this crisis . . ." Ibid., 459–460.

p. 54,   "August 28 will . . ." James Haskins, *The March on Washington* (New York: HarperCollins, 1993), 69.

p. 56,   "Nigger lover . . ." Euchner, *Nobody Turn Me Around,* 64.

p. 56,   "hook man would . . ." Patrick Henry Bass, *Like a Mighty Stream: The March on Washington, August 28, 1963* (Philadelphia: Running Press, 2002), 96.

p. 56,   "We will march . . ." Tom Engelhardt, *The End of Victory Culture: Cold War America and the Disillusioning of a Generation* (Amherst: University of Massachusetts Press, 2007), 167–168.

p. 57,   "believe it would . . ." Branch, *Parting the Waters,* 871.

p. 57,   "You are committing . . ." Bass, *Like a Mighty Stream,* 95.

p. 57,   "announced that the . . ." Branch, *Parting the Waters,* 872.

p. 57,   "volley after volley . . ." "The March in Washington," *Time,* http://time-demo.newscred.com/article/9bd69ea3626c76d7a9b0d771234f278c.html/edit.

p. 57,   "marchers to bring . . ." Ibid.

pp. 57, 60 "felt that he . . ." Bass, *Like a Mighty Stream,* 94.

p. 60,   "I guess you . . ." Fred Powledge, "Alabamians Gay on Bus Journey," *New York Times,* August 28, 1963.

p. 60,   "She said have . . ." Ibid.

p. 60,   "You forget we . . ." Ibid.

p. 60, "because my people . . ." Lerone Bennett, Jr., "The Day They Marched," *Ebony*, October 1999, http://findarticles.com/p/articles/mi_m1077/ is_12_54/ai_55982859/.

p. 61, "will be orderly . . ." John E. Hansan, "March on Washington, D.C.," The Social Welfare History Project, http://www.socialwelfarehistory. com/events/march-on-washington/.

p. 61, "When [our] train . . ." Bass, *Like a Mighty Stream*, 99.

CHAPTER 5
A Quarter-Million Strong

p. 63, "[We were] riding . . ." Euchner, *Nobody Turn Me Around*, 81.

p. 64, "I've never been . . ." Ibid.

p. 64, "I saw people . . ." Ibid.

p. 64, "We are here . . ." Haskins, *The March on Washington*, 80.

p. 66, "get a taxi . . ." Fred Powledge, *Free at Last? The Civil Rights Movement and the People Who Made It* (Boston: Little, Brown and Company, 1992), 539.

p. 66, "Yes, how many . . ." "Bob Dylan Blowin' In The Wind Lyrics," LyricsFreak, http://www.lyricsfreak.com/b/bob+dylan/ blowin+in+the+wind_20021159.html.

p. 67, "The people are . . ." "Marcher From Alabama," *New York Times*, August 29, 1963.

p. 67, "My God, they're . . ." John Lewis with Michael D'Orso, *Walking with the Wind* (Boston: Houghton Mifflin Harcourt, 1999), 223.

p. 70, "John, I know . . ." Branch, *Parting the Waters*, 879.

p. 72, "Fellow Americans, we . . ." Juan Williams, "A Great Day in Washington," *Crisis*, July/August 2003, 28.

p. 72, "When we leave . . ." "For Jobs and Freedom: The Leaders Speak," *Crisis*, August/September 1973, 228.

p. 72, "Yes, we come to march . . ." Ibid., 229.

p. 73, "In good conscience . . ." "Original Draft of SNCC Chairman John Lewis' Speech to the March," Civil Rights Movement Veterans, http:// www.crmvet.org/info/mowjl.htm.

p. 73, "The black masses . . ." Ibid.

p. 76, "got sort of . . ." Garth E. Pauley, "John Lewis, 'Speech at the March on Washington' (August 28, 1963)," *Voices of Democracy 5* (2010): 18–36, umvod.files.wordpress.com/2011/01/pauley-lewis-ii.pdf.

p. 76, "The speech still . . ." Lewis, *Walking with the Wind*, 227.

p. 76, "[When I] looked . . ." Ibid.

p. 76,   "We must have . . ." "Actual SNCC Chairman John Lewis' Speech to the March," Civil Rights Movement Veterans, http://www.crmvet.org/info/mowjl2.htm.

p. 76,   "To those who . . ." Ibid.

p. 76,   "As I stepped . . ." Lewis, *Walking with the Wind*, 228.

p. 78,   "fair employment . . ." "For Jobs and Freedom: The Leaders Speak," *Crisis*, August/September 1973, 230.

p. 78,   "To me, the . . ." Ibid.

p. 78,   "I was meant . . ." "James L. Farmer Biography," CORE, http://www.core-online.org/History/james_farmer_bio.htm.

p. 79,   "From a South . . ." "For Jobs and Freedom: The Leaders Speak," *Crisis*, August/September 1973, 231.

p. 79,   "Some of us . . ." Ibid.

p. 79,   "We will not . . ." "Getting to the March on Washington, August 28, 1963," U.S. Department of Transportation, http://www.fhwa.dot.gov/highwayhistory/road/s33.cfm.

p. 79,   "die three times . . ." "For Jobs and Freedom: The Leaders Speak," *Crisis*, August/September 1973, 232.

p. 80,   "It is simply . . ." Ibid., 237.

p. 80,   "Now the President's . . ." Ibid.

p. 80,   "People fumbled for . . ." Branch, *Parting the Waters*, 881.

pp. 80–81, "button-down men in . . ." Peter Guralnick, *Dream Boogie: The Triumph of Sam Cooke* (New York: Hachette Digital, 2005), 511.

p. 81,   "I wish I . . ." Euchner, *Nobody Turn Me Around*, 188.

p. 81,   "When I was . . ." For Jobs and Freedom: The Leaders Speak," *Crisis*, August/September 1973, 238.

p. 81,   "America must not . . ." Ibid.

p. 82,   "Hip, hip . . . hooray! . . ." Euchner, *Nobody Turn Me Around*, 191.

p. 82,   "The next president . . ." Ibid.

CHAPTER 6
"Free at Last! Free at Last!"

p. 85,   "*I* am happy . . ." "Martin Luther King—I Have A Dream Speech—August 28, 1963," YouTube, http://www.youtube.com/watch?v=smEqnnklfYs.

p. 86,   "One hundred years . . ." King, "I Have a Dream," AmericanRhetoric, http://www.americanrhetoric.com/speeches/mlkihaveadream.htm.

p. 86,   "America has given . . ." Ibid.

p. 86,   "Right on . . ." Branch, *Parting the Waters*, 881.

p. 86,   "by any means . . ." "By Any Means Necessary," YouTube, http://www.youtube.com/watch?v=M4DlfEQ7cyk.

p. 86,   "And those who . . ." King, "I Have a Dream," AmericanRhetoric, http://www.americanrhetoric.com/speeches/mlkihaveadream.htm.

p. 86,   "Let us not . . ." Ibid.

p. 89,   "we will not . . ." Ibid.

p. 89,   "I say to . . ." Ibid.

p. 89,   "I have a dream that one . . ." Ibid.

p. 89,   "I have a dream that my . . ." Ibid.

p. 90,   "My country 'tis . . ." Ibid.

p. 90,   "Let freedom ring . . ." "Martin Luther King—I Have A Dream Speech—August 28, 1963," YouTube, http://www.youtube.com/watch?v=smEqnnklfYs.

p. 91,   "we will be . . ." Ibid.

BIBLIOGRAPHY

"Actual SNCC Chairman John Lewis' Speech to the March." Civil Rights Movement Veterans. http://www.crmvet.org/info/mowjl2.htm.

AfricaWithin.com. http://www.africawithin.com/malcolmx/malcolm_speaks. htm.

"The Ballot or the Bullet." Social Justice Speeches. http://www.edchange.org/ multicultural/speeches/malcolm_x_ballot.html.

(Baltimore) *Afro-American*, September 7, 1963.

Bass, Patrick Henry. *Like a Mighty Stream: The March on Washington, August 28, 1963*. Philadelphia: Running Press, 2002.

Bennett Jr., Lerone. "Masses Were March Heroes." *Ebony*, November 1963.

_____. "The Day They Marched." *Ebony*, October 1999. http://findarticles. com/p/articles/mi_m1077/is_12_54/ai_55982859/.

Berry, Deborah Barfield. "Witnesses to King's 'Dream' speech recall unforgettable day." ClarionLedger.com. http://www.clarionledger.com/ article/20110825/NEWS/111010018/Witnesses-King-s-Dream-speech-recall-unforgettable-day.

"Beyond Vietnam—A Time to Break Silence." AmericanRhetoric. http://www. americanrhetoric.com/speeches/mlkatimetobreaksilence.htm.

"Bob Dylan Blowin' In The Wind Lyrics." LyricsFreak. http://www.lyricsfreak. com/b/bob+dylan/blowin+in+the+wind_20021159.html.

"The Bonus Army." Eyewitness to History.com. http://www.eyewitnesstohistory. com/snprelief4.htm.

Branch, Taylor. *At Canaan's Edge: America in the King Years, 1965-68*. New York, Simon & Schuster, 2006.

_____. *Parting the Waters: America in the King Years, 1954-63*. New York: Simon & Schuster, 1988.

"By Any Means Necessary." YouTube. http://www.youtube.com/ watch?v=M4DlfEQ7cyk.

"A Call for Unity." http://en.academic.ru/dic.nsf/enwiki/870259.

Carson, Clayborne, primary consultant. *Civil Rights Chronicle: The African-American Struggle for Freedom*. Lincolnwood, Ill.: Legacy Publishing, 2003.

Darden, Joe, et al. *Detroit: Race and Uneven Development*. Philadelphia: Temple University Press, 1990.

"The Dimensions of a Complete Life." The Martin Luther King, Jr. Research and Education Institute. http://mlk-kpp01.stanford.edu/index.php/ encyclopedia/documentsentry/the_dimensions_of_a_complete_life_sermon_ at_dexter_avenue_baptist_church.

Editorial. *New York Amsterdam News*, September 7, 1963.

———. *Washington Post*, August 29, 1963.

Elliott, Debbie. "Wallace in the Schoolhouse Door." NPR, June 11, 2003. http://www.npr.org/2003/06/11/1294680/wallace-in-the-schoolhouse-door.

Engelhardt, Tom. *The End of Victory Culture: Cold War America and the Disillusioning of a Generation*. Amherst: University of Massachusetts Press, 2007.

Euchner, Charles. *Nobody Turn Me Around: A People's History of the 1963 March on Washington*. Boston: Beacon Press, 2010.

"For Jobs and Freedom: The Leaders Speak." *Crisis*, August/September 1973.

Garrow, David J. *Bearing the Cross: Martin Luther King, Jr., and the Southern Christian Leadership Conference*. New York: HarperCollins, 2004.

"Getting to the March on Washington, August 28, 1963." U.S. Department of Transportation. http://www.fhwa.dot.gov/highwayhistory/road/s33.cfm.

"Give Us the Ballot." The Martin Luther King, Jr. Research and Education Institute. http://mlk-kpp01.stanford.edu/index.php/kingpapers/article/give_us_ the_ballot_address_at_the_prayer_pilgrimage_for_freedom/.

Guralnick, Peter. *Dream Boogie: The Triumph of Sam Cooke*. New York: Hachette Digital, 2005.

Hansan, John E. "March on Washington, D.C." The Social Welfare History Project. http://www.socialwelfarehistory.com/events/march-on-washington/.

Hansen, Drew D. *The Dream: Martin Luther King, Jr., and the Speech That Inspired a Nation*. New York: HarperCollins, 2005.

Haskins, James. *The March on Washington*. New York: HarperCollins, 1993.

Huie, William Bradford, to Dan Mich. October 17, 1955, page 1, in Huie Papers at Ohio State University.

"I've Been to the Mountaintop." AmericanRhetoric. http://www. americanrhetoric.com/speeches/mlkivebeentothemountaintop.htm.

"James L. Farmer Biography." CORE. http://www.core-online.org/History/ james_farmer_bio.htm.

"John F. Kennedy: Inaugural Address." AmericanRhetoric. http://www. americanrhetoric.com/speeches/jfkinaugural.htm.

"John F. Kennedy: The American Promise to African Americans." Encyclopedia Britannica. http://www.britannica.com/presidents/article-9116924.

Kenworthy, E. W. "Civil Rights Bill Passed, 73-27." *New York Times*, June 19, 1963. http://www.nytimes.com/learning/general/onthisday/big/0619. html#article.

King Jr., Martin Luther. "I Have a Dream." AmericanRhetoric. http://www. americanrhetoric.com/speeches/mlkihaveadream.htm.

_____. *Stride Toward Freedom: The Montgomery Story*. Boston: Beacon Press, 2010.

"Letter From a Birmingham Jail." *Crisis*, November 1982.

Lewis, John, with Michael D'Orso. *Walking with the Wind*. Boston: Houghton Mifflin Harcourt, 1999.

"Lyndon B. Johnson: Voting Rights Act Address." http://www. greatamericandocuments.com/speeches/lbj-voting-rights.html.

"Mahalia Jackson—How I Got Over Lyrics." http://www.songlyrics.com/ mahalia-jackson/how-i-got-over-lyrics/.

Marable, Manning, and Leith Mullings. *Let Nobody Turn Us Around*. Lanham, Md.: Rowman and Littlefield, 2009.

"The March in Washington." *Time*. http://time-demo.newscred.com/article/9bd 69ea3626c76d7a9b0d771234f278c.html/edit.

March on Washington for Jobs and Freedom. Newsletter #2.

"Marcher From Alabama." *New York Times*, August 29, 1963.

"Martin Luther King—I Have A Dream Speech—August 28, 1963." YouTube. http://www.youtube.com/watch?v=smEqnnklfYs.

Napolitano, Andrew P. *Dred Scott's Revenge: A Legal History of Race and Freedom in America*. Nashville: Thomas Nelson, 2009.

New York Times, August 29, 1963.

"News Conference 58." John F. Kennedy Presidential Library and Museum. http://www.jfklibrary.org/Research/Ready-Reference/Press-Conferences/News-Conference-58.aspx.

"November 27, 1963." Lyndon Baines Johnson Library & Museum. http://www.lbjlib.utexas.edu/johnson/kennedy/Joint%20Congress%20Speech/speech.htm.

"Original Draft of SNCC Chairman John Lewis' Speech to the March." Civil Rights Movement Veterans. http://www.crmvet.org/info/mowjl.htm.

Parks, Gordon. "Whip of Black Power." *Life*, May 19, 1967.

Pauley, Garth E. "John Lewis, 'Speech at the March on Washington' (August 28, 1963)." *Voices of Democracy 5* (2010): 18–36. umvod.files.wordpress.com/2011/01/pauley-lewis-ii.pdf.

Powledge, Fred. "Alabamians Gay on Bus Journey." *New York Times*, August 28, 1963.

_____. *Free at Last? The Civil Rights Movement and the People Who Made It*. Boston: Little, Brown and Company, 1992.

"Radio and Television Report to the Nation on the Situation at the University of Mississippi, September 30, 1962." John F. Kennedy Presidential Library and Museum. http://www.jfklibrary.org/Research/Ready-Reference/JFK-Speeches/Radio-and-Television-Report-to-the-Nation-on-the-Situation-at-the-University-of-Mississippi.aspx.

"Reasons for the March." *Crisis*, October 1963.

Reed, Roy. "The Big Parade: On the Road to Montgomery." *New York Times*, March 21, 1965. http://www.nytimes.com/learning/general/onthisday/big/0321.html.

Rieder, Jonathan. *The Word of the Lord Is Upon Me: The Righteous Performance of Martin Luther King, Jr.* Boston: Harvard University Press, 2008.

"Selma to Montgomery (1965)." The Martin Luther King, Jr. Research and Education Institute. http://mlk-kpp01.stanford.edu/index.php/encyclopedia/encyclopedia/enc_selma_to_montgomery_march/.

"Speech at the Great March on Detroit." The Martin Luther King, Jr. Research and Education Institute. http://mlk-kpp01.stanford.edu/index.php/encyclopedia/documentsentry/doc_speech_at_the_great_march_on_detroit/.

Washington, James M., ed. *A Testament of Hope: The Essential Writings and Speeches of Martin Luther King, Jr.* New York: HarperCollins, 1991.

"What We Demand." *March on Washington for Jobs and Freedom* (newsletter).

"When we leave . . ." "For Jobs and Freedom: The Leaders Speak." *Crisis*, August/September 1973.

Wilkins, Roy, with Tom Mathews. *Standing Fast: The Autobiography of Roy Wilkins.* Cambridge, Mass.: Da Capo Press, 1994.

Williams, Juan. "A Great Day in Washington." *Crisis*, July/August 2003.

_____. *Eyes on the Prize.* New York: Penguin, 2002.

Xifaras Clark, Gloria. Interview with Wilbur Colum, Mississippi Oral History Program, McCain Library and Archives.

Zinn, Howard. *SNCC: The New Abolitionists.* Boston: Beacon Press, 1964.

http://www.pbs.org/wgbh/amex/eyesontheprize/story/08_washington.html
PBS's *American Experience* documentary, *Eyes on the Prize*, features a segment on the 1963 March, including access to the text of Martin Luther King's "I Have a Dream" speech.

http://openvault.wgbh.org/collections/march-march-on-washington
Audio and transcript of twelve of fifteen hours of coverage of the March on Washington for Jobs and Freedom by The Educational Radio Network (ERN).

http://www.kingcenter.org/
The King Center, established by Coretta Scott King in 1968.

http://www.auctr.edu/mlkcollection
The Martin Luther King Jr. Collection at Morehouse College.

http://www.ourdocuments.gov/doc.php?flesh=true&doc=96
The official program for the March on Washington.

INDEX

INDEX

PHOTO CREDITS